Institutional Injustice

Institutional Injustice
The Family Courts at work

Martin Mears

Illustrations by
Jilly

Civitas: Institute for the Study of Civil Society
London
Registered Charity No. 1085494

First Published January 2006

Text © Martin Mears 2005
Illustrations © Jilly 2005

The Institute for the Study of Civil Society 2005
77 Great Peter Street
London SW1P 2EZ
Civitas is a registered charity (no. 1085494)
and a company limited by guarantee, registered in
England and Wales (no. 04023541)

Email: books@civitas.org.uk

ISBN-10   1-903 386 48-9
ISBN-13 978-1-903 386 48-9

Independence: The Institute for the Study of Civil Society
(CIVITAS) is a registered educational charity (No. 1085494) and
a company limited by guarantee (No. 04023541). CIVITAS is
financed from a variety of private sources to avoid over-reliance
on any single or small group of donors.

All publications are independently refereed. All the Institute's
publications seek to further its objective of promoting the
advancement of learning. The views expressed are those of the
authors, not of the Institute.

Typeset by Typetechnique, London W1

Printed in Great Britain by
Hartington Litho Limited

… the law is a ass—a idiot… the law is a bachelor; and the worst I wish the law is, that his eye may be opened by experience.

Mr Bumble in *Oliver Twist* by Charles Dickens

Contents

Author

Martin Mears read law at Wadham College, Oxford and is a practising solicitor. He is a well known legal journalist who has contributed, *inter alia*, to *The Times, Daily Telegraph* and *Spectator*. He is a past editor of the Law Society's *Client Care Guide* and member of the Law Society's Family Law Committee. In 1995 Martin Mears was the first person to be elected President of the Law Society by the whole solicitors' profession.

Note

FLR = Family Law Reports
All ER = All England Law Reports

1

Introduction

Fifty years ago the average citizen could easily pass his whole life without contact with the legal system. Unless you were a criminal or one of the small minority of car owners you would be unlikely ever to set foot in a magistrates court. In the civil courts most of the litigants were businessmen or corporations (public or private). Divorce was disreputable territory, inhabited by co-respondents in suede shoes and seedy enquiry agents peering through bedroom windows. It was not something the respectable went in for.

If you got the sack you shrugged your shoulders and looked for another job. Work might be getting you down but it didn't occur to you to sue someone for stress. There were no officially designated victim classes whose grievances would eventually come to sustain a whole industry of tribunals, officials and lawyers.

That was 50 years ago. Today it would be a very unusual person who did not at some time or other run up against the courts or the lawyers. Employment law which once (under the archaic description 'Master and Servant') impinged only on the peripheries of the legal profession now engrosses armies of specialists who practise in separately designated courts (employment tribunals). Anyone who now loses his job is furnished with a formidable array of legal weaponry to direct against his former employer. This is particularly so if it can be alleged with any plausibility that the real reason for the dismissal was that the employee was female/black/disabled/homosexual/lesbian. Or perhaps the employer harboured secret prejudices on account of the employee's religious beliefs?

If the discrimination industry's expansion has been

phenomenal, the growth of the personal injury/negligence sector has also been impressive. This industry's philosophy was well summed up in the notorious slogan of one of the new breed of Claims Assessors, 'Where there's blame there's a claim'. In practice almost any misfortune can beget a claim since no accident occurs without at least a modicum of fault on someone's part.

Resort to the courts has been further promoted by the 1999 Access to Justice Act which legalised no-win-no-fee agreements. Before then such agreements were unlawful, forbidden by the lawyers' professional rules and generally regarded as distasteful ambulance chasing in the American mode. No longer.

The 1949 Legal Aid Act likewise assisted in establishing the litigation culture. In the 1980s the then Lord Chancellor Hailsham spoke of the legal aid budget as 'out of control'. This was no surprise. When people are given, as they believe, a blank cheque to litigate, they litigate.

The European Union and the 1998 Human Rights Act have between them created yet another impetus to litigate. The 1998 Act incorporated the European Convention on Human Rights into English domestic law. By virtue of British membership of the European Union, United Kingdom courts are also required to apply Union law as interpreted by the European Court of Justice or otherwise.

It is, however, the family courts where the average citizen is most likely to find himself a litigant, willing or unwilling. In 2004 there were more than half as many divorces as marriages (156,814 and 286,129 respectively) in England and Wales. In nearly all marital breakdowns there is property to be divided and/or spousal/child support claims and children issues to be resolved. Even the simplest and most amicable divorce involves expensive visits to the lawyers. And, of course, many of the connected financial and children disputes are far from straightforward or amicable.

The net effect of all these developments is that the courts and the lawyers play a hugely greater role in the affairs of society than they did. The Human Rights Act made the courts into quasi-legislators. The Act's supporters sometimes deny this but the truth was plainly admitted by a Law Lord, Lord Hope: 'It is now plain that the incorporation of the European Convention on Human Rights into our domestic law will subject the entire legal system to a fundamental process of review and, *wherever necessary, reform by the judiciary*'.[1] (Emphasis added.)

If the judges are going to occupy this pre-eminent position, it is important that we should at least know what kind of men and women they are, what kind of laws they are making (or, as they would say, interpreting or clarifying) for our benefit and what kind of judicial quasi-legislation we may expect in the future. In the realm of family law, in particular, we need to be concerned about the quality of judicial decision making. This has acquired a dismal reputation over the years, but is that reputation justified?

---

[1] *R-v-DPP* ex parte Kebilene (200) 2AC 326.

2

Yesterday's Lawyers

The traditional English judge was characterised by George Orwell as a reactionary and ferocious old brute whose only virtue was that he did not take bribes. The Lord Chief Justice Goddard (who retired in 1958) fitted this stereotype perfectly. Of him it was alleged by his enemies that he obtained a perverted thrill from passing the death sentence. In Goddard's day, of course, to don the black cap would be something most High Court judges would expect to do at some time in their careers. Very few of them seem to have been much troubled by this.

Goddard himself was in a mainstream tradition which embraced his equally reactionary predecessor Lord Chief Justice Hewart. Mr Justice Wilkes acquired his niche in history as the judge who sentenced Oscar Wilde to two years hard labour and expressed regret that it couldn't be more.

Compared to Goddard and judges like him, Alfred Denning, who was Master of the Rolls (in effect president of the Court of Appeal) from 1963 to 1982, was considered an enlightened radical and greatly admired as such by the younger generation of lawyers. In truth, however, Denning's radicalism amounted to little more than an itch to legislate, to 'interpret' rules in the way he thought they should have been made. He was firmly convinced that judges like himself were far better fitted to make laws than mere politicians. His judgements had a homely unpompous (and at the time very untypical) style which gave them an air of man-o'the-people sagacity. Denning was notable as an exponent of the doctrine that in resolving a property dispute between husband and wife the court should have in effect a free hand to do whatever it thought right regardless of statute or precedent (more of this later).

Lord Denning's progressive credentials were, alas, irretrievably damaged by his judgement in the Birmingham Six case. This was one of the most famous of the miscarriages of justice which disfigured the legal system in the 1970s and '80s. The Six were Irishmen who had been arrested after a particularly atrocious IRA atrocity (the Birmingham pub bombing). Following their arrest they made full confessions. It was eventually accepted that these confessions had been beaten out of them by the police and this was the main ground of their appeal. Denning rejected the appeal in words which became notorious. Even if these men were innocent, he seemed to be saying, it was better that they should remain in prison rather than that the system should be brought into disrepute by an acknowledgement that their conviction had been wrong. This is a judicial mindset typical of Denning's generation.

If the traditional judge was reactionary, so was the legal profession from which he emerged. In private life the Goddards and Hewarts were often affable chaps, enjoying a glass of port and popular with their former colleagues at the Bar whose mindset was much the same as theirs. Most solicitors, likewise, were small and large 'c' Conservatives. Their professional body, the Law Society, occupied clubland like premises from which women were long excluded. The Society's contribution to whatever legal debate happened to be taking place was almost invariably to defend the status quo.

Fifty years ago neither the judges nor the legal profession as a whole saw any need to change society. Certainly they had no wish to be innovators themselves. Lord Denning was almost alone in his judicial activism (originally not an English but a transatlantic term). Time and again the courts, confronted with an unsatisfactory law, emphasised that it was for Parliament and not for them to change it.

When did the climate change? The process, naturally, was a very gradual and at first almost an imperceptible one. The first signs were visible in the mid-1980s. The Conservatives had been in power for five years and Arthur Scargill's National Union of Miners had suffered an unprecedented and overwhelming defeat at the hands of Margaret Thatcher. Mrs Thatcher was loathed by the old left but hardly less so by 'social liberals' and so called One-Nation Conservatives. By the mid-nineties Mrs Thatcher had gone, but the government was visibly exhausted, scandal-prone and enormously unpopular. There remained no kind of chic in being a Tory and the tides of *bien pensant* opinion and fashion were plainly flowing the other way. At the same, time positions of power and authority were in the law, as elsewhere, coming to be occupied by people whose notions, prejudices and outlook had been acquired in the radical sixties and seventies. In the 1980s a retired Law Lord, Templeman, thought that fewer than 10-15 per cent of the judges were Labour supporters. The new breed of High Court judge, on the contrary, might harbour a sentimental regard for Mr Scargill or (like Tony Blair himself) pass an evening strumming the guitar acquired during his student days.

3

Today's Lawyers

In the past 20 years or so the outlook of the whole British establishment has undergone radical change. During that time the minority mindset has become that of the majority, a mindset embracing a package of opinions and assumptions which their holders regard as almost self-evidently true. This phenomenon we know as political correctness. The term is now used pejoratively but in its dictionary definition it provides a neutral and accurate description of the modern establishment's culture: 'Conformity to a prevailing body of liberal opinion esp. in avoiding language, behaviour etc. which might conceivably be regarded as discriminatory or pejorative to racial or cultural minorities or as reflecting undesirable implicit assumptions' (Oxford Reference Dictionary). The key words in this definition are 'conformity', 'might *conceivably* be regarded' and 'undesirable.'

Political correctness is a quasi-religion in its assumption that there is a right and wrong way of looking at the world, that the right way can readily be identified by people of goodwill and that those who fail to identify it demonstrate ignorance or malice. This quasi-religion is obsessed with discrimination whether of race, gender, 'sexual orientation' or otherwise. The modern legal establishment shares and promotes this obsession.

Look, for instance, at the Bar. During the past ten years nearly all Bar chairmen have subscribed to the liberal consensus. A number of them have been overt Labour supporters. Three of these (Grabiner, Brennan and Goldsmith, the current Attorney General) have actually gone to the Lords as Labour peers.

In September 1995 the Bar Council issued its Equality

Code. This document is a model of its kind. It gives examples of the way in which the unwary might unwittingly fall into sin. To require high A-Level scores from a job applicant, for instance, might be 'indirectly discriminatory as mature women and ethnic minorities are more likely to have been admitted onto degree courses via access courses and will therefore not have A-levels'.

Neither should barristers' chambers insist that applicants for pupilage should have a good degree. That discriminates against ethnic minorities who, it was alleged, tend not to have good degrees. Naturally a requirement that an applicant should have an Oxbridge degree would be objectionable.

The document goes on to warn against asking women about their marital status or plans to have children. Such questions would stem from 'a stereotypical view of a woman's role in marriage'. It is even dangerous to ask a candidate about his/her outside activities as 'this could have an indirectly discriminatory impact on applicants with family responsibilities or an ethnic minority applicant whose outside activities may conform to an unfamiliar set of cultural norms'. 'Informal methods of recruitment' are taboo as savouring of old boy networks.

In interviewing an applicant you must not assume the sex of an interviewee's partner and a list is given of questions to avoid. This includes the following:

- 'What are your plans for a family?'
- 'What does your spouse do?'
- 'Do you think you will be able to fit in?'
- 'Would you defend someone accused of homophobic harassment or attack?' (It is not clear what the 'correct' answer is here.)

It is hard to realise that the Equality Code is the product of a profession which not long ago was a by-word for stuffed shirt fogyism. The document could have been issued without amendment by any of the so-called loony left local authorities of the 1980s. (We no longer hear about loony leftism, of course, this having now become mainstream opinion.)

In PC zealotry the Law Society has been outdistanced by the Bar Council, but the Society at least started earlier. For years it had its highly politicised equal opportunities committee and in 1995 it published its own Discrimination Code. In 1999 one of its council members was formally reported to and rebuked by the Office for the Supervision of Solicitors for making disrespectful comments about homosexuality during a council debate.

Most recently the Society has ruled that no-one can take his place as an elected member of its ruling council until he has undergone compulsory 'equality and diversity' training, i.e. orthodoxy indoctrination. Not a single member, it appears, has objected to this profoundly undemocratic decree. The Society also requires all its internal documentation to be both discrimination and human rights compliant. A council paper setting out proposals for new storage facilities, for instance, would need a certificate that the scheme had no equal opportunities/human rights implications (or otherwise as the case might be).

From time to time journalists go to the Law Society's Chancery Lane headquarters and make much copy in describing the fusty atmosphere and the grimy oleographs of departed worthies, the invariable message being that this is a last bastion of white male traditionalism. In the same way an observer present at the opening session of the States General in 1789 and seeing the delegates with their wigs and knee breeches might have imagined that nothing had much changed or was likely to change. Old forms disguise new realities.

At the Law Society as elsewhere the catchphrase 'celebrating equality and diversity' conceals the fact that, in the scale of the liberal orthodoxy, some groups count as more equal than others and not all diversity is equally worthy of celebration. The Society's current diary, for instance, contains a list of 'public and religious holidays' which includes the following:

Birthday of Guru Gobind Singh: 5th January
Muslin New Year: 22nd February
Martyrdom of Guru Arjan: 24th June
Lailat-ul-Qadr: 11th November
Diwalis, Lakshmi Puja: 12th November

The list does not include Christmas or any other Christian feast day.

Such is the cultural climate of the lawyers' professional bodies. Very many senior barristers and solicitors sit as part-time judges or employment tribunal chairmen with the expectation of occupying full judicial office. It would, therefore, be surprising if the mindset displayed by the Bar Council and Law Society were not mirrored among the judiciary. So it turns out.

A year or two ago, for instance, the Lord Chief Justice, Lord Woolf, rebuked a group of large City of London law firms for 'elitism'. The firms had co-operated in imposing particularly stringent academic requirements for prospective trainees. For Lord Woolf (as with the Bar's equality document) the sin of elitism is committed by valuing perceived intellectual capacity over the factors of class, race, gender and 'orientation'. Recently the Lord Chancellor (to the dismay, paradoxically, of Lord Woolf) announced the erosion of the entry requirements for judicial appointments in the interests of increased 'diversity'.

Following the Bar's equality document, the Judicial Studies board produced its own equal treatment *Bench Book*. This also is a document of impeccable liberal orthodoxy running to hundreds of pages. The *Bench Book's*

approach is the now familiar one. It declares, for instance, that 'judges need to understand the nature of indirect or institutional discrimination and the way it can affect what takes place in court'. That institutional racism actually exists in the legal system and elsewhere is, of course, taken for granted. The *Bench Book* goes on to warn judges that they should be 'alert in all their cases to possible racial motivation that may have been missed by police or the CPS'—a sufficiently unlikely event since the police and the CPS are subject to their own intensive equality and diversity education.

As with the Bar's equality document, the *Bench Book* accepts at face value and without criticism 'research' whose theme is that black defendants get a raw deal from the criminal system.

No less than the Bar document, the *Bench Book* illustrates the O.R.D. definition of political correctness as avoiding language 'which might conceivably' be regarded as discriminatory or 'as reflecting undesirable implicit assumptions'. It tells the reader, for instance, that it is unsafe to use the words 'black' or 'coloured' as someone somewhere might be offended by them. It notes that the phrase 'visible minorities' might seem neutral enough but in reality is 'problematic' as 'seemingly implying the existence of invisible minorities'.

The term 'West Indian' is 'inappropriate' as carrying a 'colonial overtone'. The use of the word 'British Asian' requires 'great sensitivity'. It is even dubious to speak of 'ethnic minorities' while 'ethnics' is 'an exclusionary expression which should certainly be avoided'.

The *Bench Book* goes on to provide glossary of terms. Thus 'kachha' is the Sikh for 'long underpants' while a chunni is a headscarf worn by Hindu and Sikh women. A Vajrajana is a 'sub-school of Maayana Buddhism in Tibet'. It is difficult to argue that information of this nature is essential for the proper conduct of court proceedings.

What we are seeing is an example of what in other contexts is called cultural cringing.

Of the *Bench Book* it may be said that, like the Bar code, it could be issued without amendment by any of the official or semi official organs of the discrimination industry.

It is, indeed, the kind of document produced (amidst almost universal ridicule) by Red Ken Livingstone in the 1980s.

This is the background which has produced the increasing flow of right-on judges, people of impeccable liberal orthodoxy. Theirs is a mindset now shared by most of their colleagues. A supposedly old-style traditionalist, Sir William Macpherson, surprised everyone with his '*we-are-all-racists*' report on the death of Stephen Lawrence. In fact he only illustrated the truism that a real establishment man will conform to the prevailing culture, whatever this happens to be.

4

Family Courts and Family Lawyers

Family judges also are the products of the current orthodoxies. They, too, have read their *Bench Book* and undergone their equality and diversity indoctrination. They, no less than the rest of us, carry their own baggage of cultural conditioning, prejudices and preconceptions. Moreover, they are very far from leaving this baggage outside the courtroom when they sit in judgement. How could it be otherwise when it never occurs to the average judge that he could be other than an impartial dispenser of pure justice according to the law?

It is in this area that judicial conditioning, prejudice and (as it seems to outsiders) sheer wrong-headedness is most blatant. Of this there is a wealth of anecdotal evidence, but since this evidence derives mainly from disgruntled litigants it tends to be discounted. Anyone who has lost a case is naturally inclined to blame the judge or 'the system'. And when he tells his sad tale there is, of course, no means of knowing that the account is accurate, or that he has told the whole story.

In looking at the attitudes of the family judges, therefore, I propose to rely only on their decisions as recorded in the Law Reports, these decisions being based on the findings of fact set out in the Reports themselves.

The power of the family courts to blight lives is immense and it is surprising that so little systematic investigation has been devoted to examining how this power is exercised. As we have seen, it is not as though only a few people are affected. There is, moreover, a movement to extend the courts' jurisdiction to unmarried cohabitants.

Who Makes the Decisions?

The vast majority of financial orders following a divorce are made by District Judges. A District Judge has jurisdiction in all cases save where the assets involved are unusually substantial or the issues particularly complex. Moreover, he has an exceptionally wide discretion. His decision can be reviewed by a Circuit Judge, but, provided it is not plainly perverse, it is unlikely to be overruled. The sheer cost of litigation, moreover, makes an appeal a last resort. In the exercise of his discretion a District Judge can deprive a party of his/her home or half his/her pension. He can order the transfer of assets representing a lifetime's work. He can impose a crippling and continuing maintenance obligation. He can, in short, impose sanctions (albeit not described as such) considerably more burdensome than a sentence of a criminal court.

Who are the King Solomons vested with this draconian jurisdiction? The answer is that the typical District Judge is a very average solicitor who has achieved very moderate success in private practice. For him his appointment will usually represent a significant increment both in salary and status. Some District Judges, of course, are capable lawyers and fair-minded people who, on the whole, do a good job. But there are many others who are obtuse or prejudiced or bad tempered (these characteristics occasionally being combined in one person). Prejudice? In one court familiar to me there were two men known to practitioners respectively as the Wives' Registrar (the old name for District Judge) and the Husbands' Registrar. If you were the husband's lawyer it was a great misfortune to find your case listed before the Wives' Registrar and vice versa. Or I recall another District Judge who himself had undergone a disagreeable divorce. The experience visibly conditioned his subsequent handling of husband/ wife disputes.

District Judges tend to be loose cannons. Even in the

same court one District Judge will be known to have very different attitudes from another. Some are wholly unpredictable.

The attitudes of the higher courts, on the other hand, are only too predictable. The Family Division of the High Court consists of a few dozen people who formerly practised as specialist family lawyers. In due course some of these judges are elevated to the Court of Appeal where, a tiny coterie, they then adjudicate husband/wife/ children appeals. It is this coterie (the same few names recurring again and again) which for all practical purposes makes family law with only formal deference to Acts of Parliament.

5

Institutional Bias: Ancient and Modern

The overriding characteristic of the law created by the coterie is an institutional bias in favour of wives/mothers and against husbands/fathers. This bias originally derived from old fashioned paternalism. For judges of Lord Denning's generation, women were weak, put-upon creatures ever in need of the active protection of chivalrous courts. This assumption went hand in hand with the notion that traditional male/female roles were part of the natural and inevitable order of things. In the leading matrimonial case of *Wachtel-v-Wachtel* ([1973] 1 All ER 829), for instance, Lord Denning laid down the rule that following a divorce a wife should receive maintenance of one third of her husband's net income rather than half on the ground that the husband would have to find 'some woman' (as he put it) to look after his house.

In the 1990s the judiciary's paternalistic attitudes were supplemented by the impact of feminism and the Bench Book/Bar code doctrine that any kind of gender 'discrimination' was the worst of all evils. In practice, this meant that virtually every one of the courts' frequent reinterpretations of the law represented a diminution in the position of husbands and an aggrandisement in that of wives. For the moment we need not consider whether these developments should be applauded or otherwise. It is undeniable that they occurred.

In children disputes the attitudes of the courts were even more wife/mother biased. This again was the result of cultural conditioning. For an old-style judge, it was axiomatic that children were a mother's business, the father's proper role being more or less confined to providing financial support. A typical judge of the older

generation, also, would have been packed off to a
boarding school at the age of eight. His subsequent
dealings with his father would have been remote and
infrequent. This explains why in the past so many family
judges have thought it strange and unreasonable of a
father to want to see his children more than once a
fortnight—'My father hardly ever saw me. It made me
what I am today. Why should it be any different with you?'

Bias and wrong headedness is (as we shall see) the
strand running through the decisions of the senior family
judges during the past 20 years. At the same time there is
an insistence that the court's discretion must not be
circumscribed in any way. One consequence of this is that
mature and responsible people, no matter how thoroughly
and well advised, are not permitted to conclude their own
binding prenuptial agreement or divorce settlement. The
court insists on its right to set the agreement/settlement
aside and to substitute an arrangement of its own. That
Parliament should continue to permit this judicial
arrogance is puzzling.

6

The Sad Tale of Mr Clark

Even among the numerous follies and injustices of the family courts, the first instance decision in *Clark-v-Clark* (1999 2 FLR 498) remains in a league of its own. Anyone who clings to the notion that these courts deserve any measure of public confidence should read the Law Report.

The facts in Clark were notorious at the time and attracted much media attention. In reciting them, however, I have disregarded the non-legal press reporting (which the judges always insist is inaccurate and unfair to them) and rely wholly on the findings summarised by Lord Justice Thorpe in the Court of Appeal.

At the time of Appeal in 1999 Mr Clark was 86 and Mrs Clark 50. Mr Clark was a retired insurance broker. The parties met at Christmas 1991 and married a few months later. In the money of the time Mr Clark was a rich man having, *inter alia*, £2 million worth of shares, £1 million on deposit and a home worth half-a-million. Following the marriage he purchased another property (Thatch Cottage) for £195,000 and spent a further £85,000 doing it up. This he transferred into the joint names of himself and his new wife. These were considerable assets at a time when property prices generally were very depressed.

The first instance judge, Mr Rodger Hayward Smith QC (a well known matrimonial specialist and editor of a leading text book), delivered an extensive judgement in which he made various findings of fact. Most importantly, he found that Mrs. Clark 'did not love her husband and she only married him for his money. She had the power to extract money from him and this is a thread running through the history'.

'She did not love her husband and she only married
him for his money'

An Inauspicious Day

In the Court of Appeal Lord Justice Thorpe described the wedding day as 'not auspicious' which was something of an understatement. 'The wife left at the start of the small reception. When she returned later she did not permit the consummation of the marriage'. The next day she left and did not thereafter permit cohabitation.

A few months later poor old Mr Clark presented a nullity petition on the grounds of non consummation. Optimism, however, soon prevailed over prudence and the petition was dismissed by consent. Thereafter, Mr Clark spent £146,000 redeeming a mortgage on his wife's own home and he paid £30,000 in settlement of her debts. Here, let us allow Lord Justice Thorpe to take up the story:

> For the following 18 months the wife lived at Thatch Cottage refusing to join her husband even when he was unwell. She barely tolerated his weekend visits. Only once did she admit him to her bedroom. Before long she relegated him to a caravan in the garden. Although the wife had persuaded the husband to purchase a London flat on the fantasy that it was to be their love nest, the [first instance] judge found that she never had any intention of staying there and had deliberately misled the husband. Not only did the wife decline cohabitation but she refused to acknowledge the existence of the marriage even to their employees in the house… However, her control of the situation enabled her to persuade the husband to spend nearly £117,000 on the renovation of a boat which she had owned before the marriage.

The Lover and the Geriatric Nursing Home

Later on Mrs Clark induced her husband to spend £28,500 on the purchase of a shop for her 19-year-old son. To finance this and other acquisitions Mr Clark sold his home in Highgate, following which Mrs Clark arranged for him to stay at a geriatric nursing home. Meanwhile, she induced him to buy another property called Wellow Park and she spent £100,000 of his money on this. Her object was to divide the property into two unequal parts, the intention being that Mr Clark would live in the smaller part which was separated from her quarters by connecting doors with locks only on her side. The first instance judge described the husband's part as 'small, dark and depressing', adding that 'the reality is that Mrs Clark did not want to live with her husband and she took every step to try to ensure that she did not... She did wish, however, to have the use of his money.'

A Little Present

The long suffering Mr Clark commenced divorce proceedings. Once again, however, they were reconciled on his wife's promise to look after him for the rest of his life. On the basis of this promise he was induced to transfer half his share portfolio to her and later the remaining half. He was also cajoled into transferring into her sole name both Wellow Park and two London flats. With her husband's money Mrs Clark then opened an ice-cream shop installing as manager a gentleman 15 years younger than herself and with whom she commenced a sexual relationship. This gentleman was moved into her part of Wellow Park. This she followed up by buying a Bentley for £38,500, telling her husband 'that she had given herself a little present for putting up with five years marriage to him'. Mr Hayward Smith went on to find that Mrs Clark had virtually made a prisoner of her husband and that 'life for him was no longer worth living'. It was not surprising that he attempted suicide by taking an overdose of sleeping pills. Eventually the old man was rescued by the police at the insistence of his family and this time the parties separated for good.

Following the separation Mr Clark offered his wife a financial package worth £592,000. That this offer should in all the circumstances have been rejected says much about the state of the law at the time. Mrs Clark was presumably advised (with justification as it turned out) that there were virtually no circumstances in which a divorcing wife need fear that the courts might send her away empty handed.

Having rejected her husband's offer Mrs Clark made an application to the court for what the lawyers quaintly call 'ancillary relief'. The hearing of the application took a full eight days with a stupendous expenditure of legal fees (another notable feature of family court justice which we shall consider in due course).

Overwhelming Psychological Need

On the conclusion of the hearing Mr Hayward Smith summarised the wife's assets at the time as amounting to just over £1 million net of tax. All these had come from Mr Clark. She herself, the judge found, had 'made a negative contribution in the sense of caring for the husband... I have no doubt that it was her behaviour that led him to attempt suicide'. At this point, the judge made a strange albeit wholly predictable leap in logic: 'However much the wife can be criticised it would be harsh in the extreme to leave her with nothing'. In the event he awarded her a package worth £552,500, of which the cost to the unfortunate Mr Clark would be £827,000.

Now, why by ordinary rules of sense and justice would it be excessively harsh to leave this wife with nothing? The judge himself had found that she had made no kind of contribution to the marriage, that she had never intended to do so, that she had married purely for money, that she had virtually imprisoned her husband, that she had driven him to attempted suicide, that she had put him in a geriatric home, that she had fleeced him partly in order to make expensive gifts to her young lover.

And in all these circumstances to leave her unrewarded would be 'harsh in the extreme'. Make of this what you can.

Leaving aside the excessive harshness, the judge provided a second reason for his Order, *viz*: 'It was always the husband's intention to be generous to her... What I seek to achieve is that, despite the findings I have made, she should leave this court with enough to have a home and an income, a little additional capital and no debts'. This is a further example of the perverted logic of the family courts—Mr Clark had at the outset been generous and had been infamously repaid for this. Nonetheless, this generosity should count against him in making the final award.

Hayward Smith's ruling was too much even for the seasoned family practitioners in the Court of Appeal to stomach. In the words of Lord Justice Thorpe 'Mrs. Clark has brought into the public domain a very discreditable chapter which otherwise had been concealed by the confidentiality and hearings in private within the family division... What would the ordinary right thinking person make of a judicial award of over £1 million to a wife guilty of this degree of misconduct?' A non-lawyer reading these words might imagine that Hayward Smith was a maverick and his thinking untypical but (as we shall see) this is far from the case.

Mrs Clark appealed against Mr Haywood Smith's Order on the ground that it did not give her enough. She said that she had 'an overwhelming psychological need to retain Wellow Park' and that two medical experts considered that unless she had it she might commit suicide. It might seem incredible in the circumstances that Mrs Clark should have thought she might do better on appeal. Considering Mr Haywood Smith's award, however, she might reasonably have considered that no outcome was too farfetched to exclude as a possibility. She had also seen how easily it is for a lady to pull a family judge's heartstrings. She had, for instance, argued that her mental state made her unfit to attend court. Three medical experts gave evidence to the contrary. Even so the judge agreed to take her evidence at home—a minor but significant psychological victory.

In the Court of Appeal Lord Justice Thorpe made the general criticism of Haywood Smith's judgement that 'the judge faltered in progressing from his findings to his conclusion'. 'Faltered'? That, one might think, is putting it a little mildly. Lord Justice Thorpe went on to emphasise not only Mrs Clark's marital behaviour but her 'litigation misconduct'. This consisted mainly of her unreasonable refusal of her husband's settlement offers with the consequence that a further £250,000 was spent by him on legal fees (what kind of justice is it that costs so much to extract?). As to the marital conduct, Lord Justice Thorpe commented that 'It would be hard to conceive anything graver. The history is as baleful as any to be found in the Family Law Reports.' Of the award itself he said 'I do not consider that on the quite extraordinary facts of this case to have left the wife with nothing would have exceeded the wide ambit of judicial discretion.'

It has to be admitted that from beginning to end Mr Clark did little to help himself and, indeed, seems to have been a glutton for punishment. Even after Haywood Smith's Order he paid an outstanding tax liability of his wife amounting to £118,638 together with her legal costs of £59,165, a total of £177,803. At the Appeal Hearing Mr Clark applied for the repayment of the £177,803. And here we discover that the Court of Appeal's logic is hardly more to be reckoned on than that of the lower court. Lord Justice Thorpe rejected the repayment application on the ground that 'An Order requiring the wife to repay such a substantial sum would be to create fertile opportunities for continuing litigation which would rob the husband of the finality he seeks'. Why so? The making of the Order requested would have imposed no obligation actually to enforce it. If Mr Clark really did want finality he could have put the Order in his pocket and done nothing.

In the end the Appeal Court gave Mrs Clark a financial package worth around £175,000. That award left her with a lump sum sufficient (at the time) to buy a home, the Bentley (apparently retrieved from the lover), a boat and a property to let. In the end not a bad result for Mrs Clark considering Haywood Smith's findings of outrageous misconduct endorsed and amplified by the Appeal Court.

In principle, if not in degree, the Court of Appeal's award seems no less illogical and unjust than Mr Haywood Smith's. How did Lord Justice Thorpe justify it? The answer is that he did not. He says merely that 'In all the circumstances I adopt the figure of £175,000 which in round terms is what the husband proposes'. But only a few paragraphs earlier Lord Justice Thorpe was saying that Mr Clark had applied for repayment of £177,803. Or in Thorpe's words, '[Mr Clark's Counsel's] submission is that we should reduce the lump sum to zero'. It appears, therefore, that in making the £175,000 award the Appeal Court was not in fact merely acceding to the husband's proposal (though admittedly the facts as recited in this part of the judgement are as confused as the judge's reasoning).

In *Clark-v-Clark* we can see the justice of the family courts in its full plumage. The Clark decision is a good starting point to look at other leading decisions of these courts.

7

Clark-v-Clark: The Background

It must not be thought that *Clark* was a maverick case. On the contrary, it was merely one in a long and continuing series of judicial imbecilities. These excesses were not inevitable. The jurisdiction of the courts is derived from Section 25 of the Matrimonial Causes Act 1973 which sets out a number of entirely rational factors to guide the court in making a financial award following a divorce. These include the income of the parties, their respective earning capacity, the length of the marriage, the contributions made by each party to the marriage ('including any contribution by looking after the home or caring for the family') and 'the conduct of each of the parties, if that conduct is such that it would in the opinion of the court be inequitable to disregard it'. Finally, the court has an overriding duty in exercising its powers to give 'first consideration' to the welfare of any children.

The Law According To Denning

Judges like Lord Denning have regarded Section 25 as giving the courts an almost unlimited discretion, though plainly this was not Parliament's intention. In *Hamlin-v-The Law Society* he expressed the doctrine thus:

> The court takes the rights and obligations of the parties altogether and puts the pieces into a mixed bag. Such pieces are the right to occupy the matrimonial home, or have a share in it, the obligation to maintain the wife and children and so forth. The court then takes out the pieces and hands them to the two parties, some to one party and some to the other. ....without paying too nice a regard to their legal or equitable rights, but simply according to what is fairest.

The implications of these words are clear enough. Until divorce we are adult citizens with defined and undoubted rights to property and income. On divorce, however, we become as children with the court assuming the role of benevolent and omniscient nanny, gathering up her charges' sweets and toys according to her own notions of fairness (notions which the children cannot always be expected to understand). Arrogant paternalism of this kind would be hard to bear in any circumstances. Exercised by judges like Lord Denning (or Mr Hayward Smith) it becomes particularly intolerable. Denning never doubted his own qualifications to be a legislator. His influence on the development of family law was immense. It was Lord Denning in the *Wachtel* case (1973) who stated what was then a novel principle:

> It has been suggested that there should be a discount in what the wife is to receive because of her supposed misconduct, guilt or blame. We cannot accept this argument. ...There will be many cases in which a wife (though once considered guilty or blameworthy) will have cared for the home and looked after the family for many years. Is she to be deprived of the benefit otherwise to be accorded to her because she may share responsibility for the breakdown with her husband? There will no doubt be a residue of cases where the conduct of one of the parties is both obvious and gross so much so that to order one party to support another whose conduct falls into this category is repugnant to anyone's sense of justice ...short of cases falling into this category, the court should not reduce its order for financial provision merely because of what was formerly regarded as guilt or blame. To do so would be to impose a fine for supposed misbehaviour in the course of an unhappy married life.

This kind of thinking soon became (as it remains) the orthodoxy of the courts. To the general public, however, its application led to outcomes which seemed flagrantly unjust. After a media and parliamentary campaign the conduct provision was in 1984 inserted into the 1973 Act. (The amendment made no difference whatever to the attitudes of the judges. Indeed, the then President of the Family Division, Sir John Arnold, insisted that the courts were already applying the law in the way intended by the amendment. It was only puzzling that Parliament should somehow have got a different idea.)

In truth the Denning doctrine, as a rational approach to matrimonial settlements, bears little examination.

Firstly, no distinction is made between a claim for a share of the capital assets and a claim for 'continuing support', i.e. maintenance. If it is, indeed, the case that a party has made a substantial contribution to the marriage over a period of years that should give him/her a vested share in the matrimonial assets and there is no reason why he/she should be deprived of that share by subsequent bad behaviour. Whether the bad behaviour had been comparatively minor or 'obvious and gross' would be wholly irrelevant.

A claim for *continuing* support is an entirely different matter. In that case behaviour ought to have the highest relevance. How can it be right that a party should repudiate all the continuing obligations of a contract (in this case the marriage contract) while insisting on receiving the continuing benefits?

The *Wachtel* doctrine is based on the general premise which, despite its plain falsity, has nonetheless been accepted by the courts ever since, *viz*: that, save in the most blatant cases (and not always even then), marital breakdown is always to be attributed to misfortune rather than bad behaviour. Or if there has been bad behaviour on one side it must be assumed that this was provoked by similar conduct on the part of the other. The courts, said Denning, should not 'impose a fine for supposed misbehaviour in the course of an unhappy married life'. Note the 'supposed'—as though there could not be any misconduct which was real and actually did result in the breakdown of the marriage.

Before we leave *Wachtel* it is worth quoting another passage from Lord Denning's judgement and then

'It is not every homicide, or attempted homicide, by a wife of a husband which necessarily involves a financial penalty'

reflecting that among lawyers he was considered one of the most progressive of English judges:

> When a marriage breaks up there will henceforward be two households instead of one. The husband will have to go out to work all day and must get some woman to look after the house—either a wife if he remarries, or a housekeeper if he does not. He will also have to provide maintenance for the children. The wife will not usually have so much expense. She may go out to work herself, but she will not usually employ a housekeeper. She will do most of the housework herself, perhaps with some help. Or she may remarry in which case her new husband will provide for her.

Stabbed!

After *Wachtel* we should not be surprised by decisions like that in *Hall-v-Hall* ([1984] FLR 631.) In this case the marriage broke down following the wife's alleged associations with other men. On this ground the husband objected to paying her continuing maintenance. His objections were, of course, brushed aside. Following the separation, however, Mrs Hall called on her estranged husband and stabbed him in the stomach with a knife. In due course she was convicted of assault. The judge held that this conduct justified a *reduction* in the wife's maintenance from £195 a month to £50 a month. The Court of Appeal upheld this Order. What if Mrs Hall had stabbed her husband a second time? Perhaps the Order would have been reduced to £25 a month. We can see from the Hall case that Mr Haywood Smith's decision in *Clark* did not fall from a clear sky.

Incitement to Murder

The Court of Appeal decision in *Evans-v-Evans* ([1989] 1 FLR 351) might on the face of it seem to suggest an unwonted outbreak of rationality. Here the parties had married in 1949 and divorced in 1953. An Order for periodical payments was made against the husband, which over the years was varied upwards. Mr Evans carried on making the payments for 35 years. Was Mrs Evans duly grateful? No, she was not. In 1985 she was convicted of inciting others to murder her former husband and sentenced to four years imprisonment. She had, it appeared, attempted to obtain a suitable hit man via a clairvoyant, offering a fee of £1,000 (saved up from the maintenance payments?). Mr Evans successfully applied for the discharge of the maintenance order and the wife appealed. In the Court of Appeal Lord Justice Balcombe rejected the appeal on the grounds that 'if the courts were in these circumstances not to discharge the Order, the public might think we had taken leave of our senses'. He went on, however, to say that 'It is not every homicide, or attempted homicide, by a wife of a husband which necessarily involves a financial penalty.' What can these extraordinary words mean other than that if Mrs Evans had been able to put together a plausible tale in mitigation, or if she had come before a more amenable judge, she could have received her maintenance until the day she or her husband died?

To no-one, of course, did it seem grotesque in itself that 35 years after the termination of a relationship one party should still be paying money to the other. And under the *Wachtel* doctrine it would make no difference that it might have been the receiving party who had walked out of the marriage.

Conduct Irrelevant? Depends Whose It Is

It is interesting to look at a decision where it was the husband who was applying for maintenance and where his conduct was raised as an issue. In *Kay-v-Kay* ([1990] 2 FLR 225) the wife had a gross income of £24,600 while the husband was living on state benefits of £50 a week. He was unable to obtain a job and called medical evidence that 'although he is not actually mentally ill he suffers from a personality disorder'. In the event the court, while awarding him a lump sum to buy a house, dismissed his maintenance claim on the ground (*inter alia*) that his condition had 'been brought about to an extent by his own conduct'. What 'conduct'? Is a personality disorder to be regarded as something you bring on yourself and for which you should properly be penalised? It is hardly conceivable that a wife's application would have been treated with similar rigour. This brings us to the general question of bias.

8

Fragrant Bias

Bias derives from prejudices, preconceptions and general cultural conditioning. In the context of 'equality and diversity' issues, the courts have no difficulty in recognising (indeed they are anxious to acknowledge) that they too can be guilty of unconscious 'stereotyping'. Judges now willingly submit themselves to training courses to rid their minds of alleged cultural clutter. Their trainers will tell them, for example, that the failure of an Afro-Caribbean witness to look the judge in the eye is for him an indication of respect not of contempt.

Until recently lay magistrates refused to grapple with the notion that a police officer might be capable of telling lies. Today's magistrates work on the assumption that officialdom knows best. A health and safety or environmental protection prosecution is presumed well founded—a heavy onus lying on the defendant to prove otherwise.

Before many employment tribunals it is difficult for an applicant to lose a discrimination claim. The tribunal's stereotypical view of the world is that employers are likely to have stereotypical and incorrect attitudes to race, gender, etc.

Meal Tickets for Life
The attitudes of the traditional family judge we have seen illustrated in the *Wachtel* case. And sufficiently archaic and offensive they now look—particularly the notion that a woman's natural and proper destiny is to look for a man for financial support. These attitudes emerge again and again in the family courts' decisions. In *Duxbury-v-Duxbury* ([1987] 1 FLR 7), for instance, Lord Justice Ackner

began his judgement with the approving statement that 'Mr Duxbury is a wealthy man and he fairly and frankly accepted that his former wife was entitled for the rest of her life to enjoy a very comfortable and even luxurious lifestyle'. He went on to add that 'Mrs Duxbury brought no capital into the marriage and during the course of the marriage was at no time engaged in any paid employment. She gave evidence to the effect, and it was not challenged, that it would in the circumstances have been considered socially quite unacceptable to have gone out to work.'

Who outside the divorce courts would regard anyone as 'entitled' to live in idle luxury for the rest of their life?

Denningism was taken to a particularly absurd conclusion in another Court of Appeal case *Whiting-v-Whiting* ([1988] 2 FLR 189). In this case the wife, following a divorce, obtained a periodical payments order. Subsequently, she qualified as a teacher and the Consent Order was reduced to a nominal amount. Following this the husband was made redundant and applied for an order for the discharge of the nominal maintenance obligation on the ground that eight years after the collapse of the marriage a financial clean break might reasonably be imposed. At the time of his application the wife earned £10,500 per annum while he had an income of only £4,500.

In theory, both parties to a marriage have a right to claim maintenance against the other. It is not, in theory, a right vested in the wife alone which should only be removed in exceptional circumstances. In *Whiting*, therefore, the application of the law as it is *in theory* would mean that a nominal maintenance order ought to have been made in favour of the husband. In the event, his application was dismissed on the ground that 'it cannot be assumed that the wife's independence will necessarily continue indefinitely. Everything turns on her continued good health and employment. If redundancy or bad health were to intervene her present good earnings might cease prematurely'.

Now, of course, this is an argument for never imposing a clean break at all, though the 1973 Act (as amended in 1984) specifically enjoins the courts to make clean break orders wherever possible. And if the wife could become ill or otherwise fall on hard times, would not the same be equally true of the husband? This being so, would not logic dictate that following every divorce each party should be left with the option to claim maintenance against the other for the remainder of their joint lives?

The fall-back rule which emerged in *Atkinson* was applied again in *Hepburn-v-Hepburn* ([1989] 1 FLR 373]). In that case the parties had been divorced after ten years of marriage. Mrs Hepburn was awarded periodical payments of £6,500 and a lump sum. She then set up home with another man and they lived together thereafter. Seven years later the husband applied for the periodical payments to be discharged because of the cohabitation. The judge made an order for nominal payments during joint lives until remarriage. The husband appealed on the ground that (*inter alia*) the wife had capacity to provide for herself and that she was in a long-term cohabitation. The Court of Appeal dismissed the appeal on the ground that cohabitation did not equate to remarriage and that the judge was 'right to hold that a court order should not pressurise an ex-wife to regularise her position with the other man so that he would assume a husband's obligation towards her'.

Hepburn was one of the numerous meal-ticket-for-life cases. *Fisher-v-Fisher* ([1989] 1 FLR 243) is another. Here, the wife, following a divorce, obtained a maintenance order and then went on to have a child by an Irishman. This gentleman prudently returned to Ireland and disappeared. Who, then, should support his child? To Mrs Fisher the answer to this question was plain. She applied to the court for an upward variation of her maintenance. The husband applied for a reduction on the ground (*inter alia*) that it was not wholly reasonable that he should

'For all we know, the child may have been conceived
in circumstances which reflect nothing but credit
on the wife'

support another man's child born after the termination of the marriage. It was only predictable that the wife's application should succeed and the husband's rejected. Again, for an egregious example of family court think we can look at the judgement of Lord Justice Nourse:

> The husband submitted that it is inequitable that a former wife who is kept at home to look after her illegitimate child, there being no financial support from the father, should be maintained at the expense of her former husband. As a general proposition, that submission is no more sustainable than his other arguments. The husband even went so far as to suggest that we should assume that the circumstances in which the child was conceived were discreditable to the wife… For all we know the child may have been conceived in circumstances which reflect nothing but credit on the wife, for example under promise of marriage from the father.

So there you are. What if the wife (in circumstances wholly creditable to her) had gone on to beget a second or a third or a fourth child? Would her former husband be expected to support these as well? Under the logic in *Fisher*, there is no reason why not.

The institutional bias (and injustice) of the courts appears in all the cases I have considered so far. Sometimes, however, this bias is so blatant as to be almost ludicrous. Everyone remembers Mr Justice Caulfield's droolings over Mary Archer in the Jeffrey Archer libel case: 'Has she fragrance… ?'

Fragrance Galore

Mrs Shirley Conran of superwoman fame made a similarly favourable impression on Mr Justice Wilson when her financial application came to court following her divorce (*Conran-v-Conran* ([1997] 2 FLR 615).

Mrs Conran was a rich woman in her own right but her husband (of Habitat fame) was even richer. The majority of his assets, however, had accrued since the marital breakdown. Mrs Conran applied to the court for a lump sum to reflect her contribution to a long marriage. In the event she was awarded £6.2 million pounds. At the time this was considered a notable victory for her and Mr Conran's public complaints were bitter. Had she brought her claim a few years later, however, she would have done even better, as we shall see.

This is Mr Justice Wilson's description of Mrs Conran's contribution:

> The wife's agreed contribution as a mother is, by itself, formidable. I have no doubt that had she not given up her full-time career in journalism when the first child was born she would have ascended the highest echelon of editorship... Then comes her contribution as a housewife over no less than 30 years, she being the primary administrator of two homes and, from 1972, also a French home. Her exceptional talents as a cook and hostess are better explained later... The husband's friends were his colleagues in business. He brought them home. The wife cooked a superb supper... What she had in abundance was flair; she is fluent in French... in 1968 the wife became the food correspondent for the *Sunday Times*. She so remained until 1981 and was, in the words of a distinguished rival, the best known food journalist in Britain... The wife wrote, co-wrote or translated no less than about ten cookery books, of which most were well received and some became a commercial success. Her translations were almost as significant as her original works: For they were translations of the seminal French books on *nouvelle cuisine*... Delicious lunches for the businessmen were organised by the wife... the home in Provence became another magnificent centre for business discussions to take place amid the exceptional hospitality which the wife with the husband was able to provide...

Wilson's Caulfieldesque panegyric continued in this vein. It would all be richly comical provided you were not the other party to the litigation. How sick Mr Conran and his lawyers must have felt.

The upshot was that Mr Justice Wilson decided that Mrs Conran needed an annual income of £230,000 with (*inter alia*) reasonable capital requirements as follows:

House in Belgravia £1,100,000
House in Dorset £800,000
Liquid capital £200,000
Chattels, jewellery, cars £400,000

Mrs Conran could reasonably argue that the lump sum she was awarded did no more than reflect a very significant contribution to a long marriage even if her virtues were not quite in the preternatural league suggested by the judgement.

There are other 'big money' cases where the wife was certainly no Shirley Conran but was nonetheless, treated by the indulgent courts as though she were.

Proud of Her Cooking

Take, for instance, the case of *A-v-A* ([1998] 2 FLR 180). Mr A was 64 and his wife 40. They had been married for 13 years. Even at the time of the marriage he was a rich man and subsequently became even richer. It was not alleged that the wife had made any financial contribution. The court had to decide what lump sum Mrs A should receive.

In delivering his judgement Mr Justice Singer struck the familiar note:

> As to her other contributions, it is common ground that in financial terms the wife made none. She neither needed to, nor was expected to. I accept that the husband would have regarded it as inappropriate for his wife, at any stage of the marriage, to be involved in any serious form of employment. For her to have done so would have been incompatible both with their position in the circles in which they moved and his requirements for her to be his homemaker and companion, to accompany him on his journeys both within and outside England and with her maternal role...

Attitudes of this kind were commonplace 30 or 40 years ago but *A-v-A* was adjudicated in 1998, years after Britain had had a female Prime Minister and when Mr Justice Singer had female colleagues in the High Court. Outside the divorce courts, would anyone in 1998 regard it as reasonable for a young woman to make no effort to make a career or achieve anything on her own account?

Mr Justice Singer continues:

> The husband told me how proud he was of her cooking and of the careful and economical manner in which she ran the household. I

have, therefore, formed the conclusion that the wife is not to be
faulted in terms of contributions to this marriage.

Bear in mind this was a husband with net assets exceeding
£100 million pounds. It is, therefore, hard to believe that
Mrs A spent very much time in filling the washing
machine or bathing the baby (the parties had only one
child).

What of Mrs A's future? The judge tells us that she had
'developed her interests and her tastes and free of the
marriage she will no doubt elaborate and refine them
further. She is likely to want to lead a more sociable life
than was her husband's preference during their marriage.
She will want to follow her own taste in furnishing and
decorating her home. She will value opportunities to
travel and for recreation...'

We are, in short, contemplating a life to be devoted to
shopping, lunching and holidaying. For these activities the
wife postulated a need for an annual budget which she
had 'pruned' to £195,000 per annum (this, of course, being
a tax free sum). Included in her stated income
requirements was an allowance of £7,000 annually for
jewellery. In the end she was left with a house worth £1.5
million, contents worth £140,000, jewellery with a value in
excess of £200,000 and a lump sum of £4.4 million.

The £4,000 per annum Labrador

Mrs A's requirements and award, however, were
modest compared with that of the wife in *F-v-F* ([1995] 2
FLR 045). The *F-v-F* award was made by Mr Justice Thorpe
who delivered the main judgement in *Clark* and whose
influence on the development of matrimonial law during
the past ten years has been immense.

In *F-v-F* the marriage was a short one, the parties
having married in 1985 and separated in 1992. The
husband had very considerable family wealth. The wife
had little and at no stage made a financial contribution. It

appears, however, that she quickly became accustomed to life as a big spender. Initially, she applied for interim maintenance and the husband offered her £220,000 per year on the basis that he would continue to provide for her rent, together with school fees. The wife on the contrary provided a budget demonstrating that she could not possibly manage on less than £539,173 per annum.

As usual, the wife found that she was knocking at an open door. Mr Justice Thorpe started off: 'It would be wrong in principle to determine the application on some broad conclusion that if the wife cannot manage at the rate of a quarter of a million a year she ought to be able to'. This said, even he found the wife's budget somewhat excessive. She had, for instance, claimed an allowance of £5,000 for 'knicknacks in the home', £12,000 for telephone expenditure, £4,000 'to keep a Labrador', £5,000 for 'stocking a drinks tray for casual visitors'. For clothes the figure was put in at £50,000 per annum. As to holidays, her budget of £50,000 for family excursions and £40,000 when she travelled alone seemed to Mr Justice Thorpe 'a bit high'. In the end, Mrs F was awarded £9 million to buy a house, £300,000 for a London flat, a life interest in a Swiss chalet, £685,000 to furnish these residences, chattels worth £100,000 and jewellery worth £300,000. For maintenance a £5 million fund was established.

Tart of Gold
I have mentioned the *Clark* decision as the apotheosis of sheer wrong headedness (not to say injustice) but the case of *C-v-C* ([1997] 2 FLR 26) runs it close. The facts here were bizarre. The parties met when the wife was working as a high-class prostitute. He was 59 at the time and she 40. Unsurprisingly, the marriage lasted less than ten months. Mrs C's financial contribution was nil. The court at first instance thought the husband had failed to give full disclosure of his financial means, but for the purposes of

'It would be wrong in principle to determine the application on some broad conclusion that if the wife cannot manage at the rate of a quarter of a million a year she ought to be able to'

its proposed order assumed that he had capital assets worth £1 million and an income of £100,000. On this basis, Mrs C was awarded a lump sum of £195,000, £19,500 per annum in periodical payments and £8,000 in child maintenance. Assuming that the husband did, in fact, have an annual income of £100,000 the maintenance payments would have represented around 40 per cent of what he received after tax—an expensive ten months for him.

The striking feature of this case (leaving aside the routine injustice) is, once again, the transparent bias displayed. This is what the first instance judge said:

> She is vulnerable to emotional reverses, resulting in depression and loss of confidence and self respect… In my view it is essential to her sense of self worth and indeed to her effective functioning that she should present herself as attractively as possible. It is important to her to be well dressed and groomed and thus she buys designer clothes, and spends considerable sums on hairdressing, fitness, make up etc. …

In reading the Law Reports one sometimes has the impression that even the judge himself senses that the magnitude of his intended award might look strange to outsiders. In that event, there is always the 'welfare of the children' to provide justification. In C-v-C the first instance judge put it in this way:

> J [the child] is, and for the foreseeable future will be, critically dependent on the quality of the physical and emotional care which the wife is able to provide for him. Should her nervous and/or physical health be undermined by financial pressures and anxieties, she will not be able to function as effectively as a mother as J's welfare requires. It is necessary for J's welfare, therefore, that the wife should have a sufficient level of financial provision and support to ensure that she is reasonably free from financial pressures and to enable her within reasonable limits to maintain the sort of appearance which is essential to her psychological and emotional wellbeing.

Or to put it more bluntly Mrs C must be provided with the money to buy her designer clothes, makeup, etc. or else the child is going to suffer. Again, one needs to follow this kind of thinking to its logical conclusion. What if Mrs C had said, 'I suffer terrible bouts of depression unless my 5 series BMW is regularly updated'?

The 1973 Act as amended in 1984 requires the court to consider whether a short-term maintenance order should be made with a view to enabling the recipient 'to adjust without undue hardship to the termination of his or her financial dependence on the other party'.

This was an exceptionally short marriage so that Mrs C could hardly have argued that she had become, as it were, addicted to dependence. Moreover, over the years she had shown some energy and enterprise in doing different jobs. She had, for instance, run a business transporting pop musicians. She had been a regional director of a cold storage business and worked for a police vehicle clamping unit. Was this not, therefore, a suitable case for a three- or five-year maintenance order (bearing in mind Mr C's financial responsibility for the child would have been ongoing in any event)? The Court of Appeal thought not. In the words of Lord Justice Ward:

> It is necessary for the court to form an opinion not only that the payee will adjust but also that the payee will have adjusted within the term that is fixed... If there is doubt about when self sufficiency will be attained, it is wrong to require the payee to apply to extend the term. If there is uncertainty about the appropriate length of the term, the proper course is to impose no term but leave the payer to seek the variation...

Again, follow the court's logic. There must always be some measure of doubt about whether a person can become financially self sufficient. This being so, there could *never* be a justification for imposing a short-term maintenance order as opposed to a continuing liability. The short-term maintenance amendment was, as I have said, inserted in 1984 following parliamentary and media protests about the reluctance of the courts to make clean-break orders. Not for the first time the response of the courts to

Parliament was, in effect, 'Pass what laws you like. We'll carry on imposing our own ideas of justice.'

As to the general question of bias, Lord Justice Ward's judgement contains this remarkable passage:

> Once the stresses of the litigation have abated then, with the benefit of the counselling she is receiving, it is to be expected that having shown herself resilient and resourceful in the past, she will begin to take up the threads of employment and seek for her own good to be financially independent of this man who has so blighted her happiness and her future.

'Blighted her happiness and her future'? Her future as what? At the time of the marriage, it will be recalled, Mrs C was working as a prostitute. And why is Lord Justice Ward not applying the Denning doctrine in this case? Marital breakdown, according to this doctrine, is a misfortune and nothing to do with 'supposed' bad behaviour.

Or can it be simply that the Denning doctrine applies when husbands complain about their wives' misconduct, but not vice versa?

There is in any event nothing in the facts as set out in the Law Report to justify the suggestion that Mr C was a cad who had blighted his wife's happiness. Earlier in his judgement Lord Justice Ward himself had said that 'the important feature of this case is that the marriage disintegrated as early as New Year's Eve 1992 for reasons *which do not matter*' (italics added).

Three Taxi-Loads of Clothes

We have seen that in justifying a wife-biased award the courts sometimes employ the 'It's really for the benefit of the children' argument. There are, however, cases where not even this bias-concealing fig-leaf is present. In the case of *E-v-E*, for instance, ([1992] FLR 233) the claimant wife had had several affairs in the course of the marriage and the judge (Mr Justice Ewbank) found as a fact that 'from

YESSS!

early 1987 the wife's contribution to the welfare of the family was negative and from 1980 it has been minimal'. At the time of the court proceedings the children were living with their father and were on poor terms with their mother who was living with another man. The judge at first instance found that in an unhappy marriage Mrs E 'compensated by spending money and retreating from her children since there was a staff to take care of everything'. Mrs E's extravagance, indeed, might have made even a family judge blink. There was, for instance, an occasion when three taxi-loads of clothes arrived at the house following one of Mrs E's spending sprees. When her husband asked for an explanation her response was that her boyfriend liked to see her well dressed. When she finally left home to set up with the gentleman friend she left behind 70 pairs of shoes, some of them in their unopened boxes and clothes which filled 20 packing cases. And so on.

When justifying his award, Mr Justice Ewbank said: 'Whatever is said about the wife and her lack of contribution, she remains and will remain the mother of these children; and the children are the grandchildren of a very rich man so it is not in their interest that she should be in straitened circumstances.' It is not easy to follow this reasoning. This was a woman who had turned her back on the marriage and upon the children. She was on bad terms with those children and living with another man. At the time of the proceedings, also, she was on the worst possible terms with the children's paternal grandparents.

What, in all the circumstances, did it matter to the children whether she was in straitened circumstances or not? Following Ewbank's reasoning to its logical conclusion, he should have given the wife ongoing maintenance—a meal-ticket for life.

9

White-v-White: New Law from Their Lordships

After the *Wachtel* decision, the House of Lords decision in *White-v-White* ([2002] FLR 281) is by far the most important case in the development of family law during the past 30 years. The decision itself provides an excellent illustration of much of what is wrong with the law both in theory and practice. Firstly, the legal costs incurred by the parties were described even by one of the Law Lords (Nicholls of Birkenhead) as 'appalling'. The estimated costs of the appeals were stated to be £530,000 and it is not clear that this figure included the costs of the earlier proceedings. What kind of justice is it that can only be obtained at this kind of price? And the costs burden in *White* was by no means unique. In *F and F*, for instance, (the case where the wife claimed £4,000 per annum for the upkeep of her Labrador) the bill was even higher. Mrs F's legal costs ultimately reached £733,521 and her husband's £770,182.

How can you knock up bills of this magnitude? Very easily. You employ specialist solicitors where the partner's charging rate is, say, £250 an hour. He is assisted by a trainee whose hourly rate is £120. At every stage of the proceedings a specialist 'junior' (which in this context means very senior) barrister is consulted. The 'junior' soon discovers that he cannot possibly handle the case aided only by a £250-an-hour solicitor and a £120-an-hour trainee. He advises that a leader (i.e. a QC) be 'taken in'. In a case where the assets are at all substantial the wife's lawyers will instruct forensic accountants whose task is to analyse the husband's finances with a view to demonstrating that he is really much richer than he appears to be. In the course of the proceedings both parties file affidavits and questionnaires and make interim applications. The haemorrhage of money is constant and stupendous. In the *F and F* case Mr Justice Thorpe (as he was at the time) gave some idea of what happens:

> On 29th September 1994 Ernst & Young and Coopers & Lybrand both completed reports and thereafter professional reports were exchanged thick and fast. The affidavits that were exchanged fill two bundles and amount to 633 pages... The solicitors' correspondence run to 1,006 pages and is contained in three files. There are nine further ring binders containing other material...

Fighting the Good Fight

Thorpe went on to comment that 'expenditure in legal costs of this magnitude is unacceptable'. He added that 'witnesses were called to issues that had little, if any, surviving relevance. I suspect that experts were instructed with a covert message to put the case as high as it could reasonably be put... The sheer bulk of the papers inevitably had an impact on the developing costs of the case. The scale of the solicitor correspondence is, in my experience, quite unprecedented'. One might think from these words that Thorpe was rebuking the learned friends and their auxiliaries. Not at all. After these apparent strictures we observe the familiar leap of logic of a family judge: 'I am not criticising any of those who have acted in the case', said Thorpe. 'The standard of the work that has been done by the solicitors on both sides and by the Bar is of the very highest. Tremendous industry has been displayed in the preparation of analysis and schedules which would not have been conceived in the days when I practised in this field. Everybody, as it seems to me, has fought this good fight according to the practices which hitherto have prevailed. All I question is whether those practices should continue to prevail and whether we do not need to change the approach and the practice so that the preparation will be undertaken more co-operatively and less contentiously and the resulting bills consequently reduced.'

The lawyers between them knock up bills exceeding £1.5 million and a judge calls this fighting the good fight! No wonder the law is so widely regarded as a racket operated for the benefit of the legal profession. Since *F-v-F*, incidentally, various procedural reforms have been introduced with a view to increasing the court's control over the progress of litigation and thereby reducing legal costs. These reforms have, if anything, actually increased the costs of an average case—an outcome which will surprise few.

Both *F-v-F* and *White-v-White* were so-called big money cases. But even where the assets consist of little more than a modest family home and a few insurance policies, the legal costs are frequently just as disproportionate. Why do rational people spend money in this way? The answer is that in the family courts the judges' discretion is so wide and so unpredictable that both parties can reasonably believe they have a good prospect of success. In the *White* case, for instance, a very experienced judge of the High Court Family Division (Mr Justice Holman) awarded the wife a package which included a lump sum of £800,000. She appealed to the Court of Appeal where equally experienced judges (including Lord Justice Thorpe) increased this sum to £1.5 million. Both parties then appealed to the House of Lords. Both were represented by well known matrimonial solicitors who in the usual way instructed specialist junior and leading counsel. Husband and wife must each, presumably, have been advised that the good fight was worth fighting. In the end, as it turned out, both were wrong since the House of Lords upheld the Court of Appeal's decision.

At the time of the litigation Mr and Mrs White had been married for over 30 years and had three children. Throughout the marriage they had carried on a dairy

*... and this is where you have to pay my lawyer
for thinking about the case in the bath ...*

farming business in partnership. Their overall net assets were approximately £4.6 million, of which part had been inherited by the husband. Rationally, this would have been a case for equal division of the assets after making an appropriate adjustment to reflect the windfall from the husband's inheritance. In the event Mr Justice Holman made his award to the wife on the basis of his assessment of her 'reasonable requirements'. This was, indeed, the basis for calculating a wife's award laid down in numerous previously decided cases. The Court of Appeal in increasing the award had regard to the wife's contribution, both to the business and the family over a long period of years.

Before the *White* case the House of Lords had not for many years been presented with the opportunity to set out firm guidelines for the resolution of matrimonial financial disputes. The opportunity was missed with the result that the *White* decision has itself resulted in a whole new generation of litigation as the lower courts have attempted to interpret and apply it.

Male-Dominated Victorian Society

In the Lords the main judgement was given by Lord Nicholls. He began by setting out the powers of the courts under the Matrimonial Causes Act 1973, noting that they are 'given a wide discretion, largely unrestricted by statutory provisions'. The pre-1973 law, he said, 'reflected the values of a male-dominated Victorian society'. Here, the discerning reader will have an inkling of what is to come. 'Male-dominated Victorian society' is a characteristic liberal establishment buzz-phrase. Sure enough Lord Nicholls goes on to warn that: 'In seeking to achieve a fair outcome, there is no place for discrimination between husband and wife and their respective roles.' And there must be no 'discrimination creeping in by the backdoor'. 'Discrimination', of course, is *the* buzz-word. It is not, however, a factor listed as relevant in the 1973 Act. Neither is it even mentioned in the leading financial provision cases pre *White-v-White*. There is, indeed, no reason why it should have been mentioned since rational application of the Section 25 factors (length of marriage, extent of contribution, needs and requirements, etc.) can and should produce an equitable result in virtually all cases.

The truth is that in mentioning discrimination as the arch sin, Lord Nicholls is doing no more than revealing himself as a typical child of his conditioning. In the year 2000 most elderly white males from affluent middle-class backgrounds subscribe instinctively to the liberal package and have also drunk deep at the well of liberal guilt (Sir William Macpherson being a prime example of the type). Lord Nicholls is merely an updated version of Lord Denning with his assumption that every divorcing man needed to find 'some woman' to housekeep for him, while every divorcing woman needed some man to provide her with financial support.

A Yardstick… But Not a Presumption

In the liberal orthodoxy it is axiomatic that any instance of gender inequality is repugnant, it being assumed that inequality is the same thing as unfairness. In *White* the Law Lords laid down a principle not to be found in the 1973 Act nor in any previous decisions. Lord Nicholls said this:

> Sometimes having carried out the statutory exercise [i.e. the evaluation of the section 25 factors], the judge's conclusion involves a more or less equal division of the available assets. More often this is not so. More often having looked at all the circumstances, the judge's decision means that one party will receive a bigger share than the other. Before reaching a firm conclusion and making an order along these lines, a judge would always be well advised to check his tentative views against the yardstick of equality of division. As a general guide, equality should be departed from only if, and to the extent that, there is good reason for doing so. The need to consider and articulate reasons for departing from equality would help the parties and the court to focus on the need to ensure the absence of discrimination.

Lord Nicholls went on to acknowledge that:

> A presumption of equal division would go beyond the permissible bounds of interpretation of Section 25... That would be so even though the presumption would be rebuttable. Whether there should be such a presumption and in respect of what assets is a matter for Parliament. It is largely for this reason that I do not accept Mr Turner's [the wife's counsel] invitation to enunciate a principle that in every case the 'starting point' in relation to a division of the assets of the husband and wife should be equality.

The rule in *White*, therefore, is that there should be no discrimination and that there should be departure from the 'yardstick of equality' only if there was a good reason for doing so. This yardstick, however, is not to be considered as a presumption or even a starting point. It would be futile to try to extract coherence from this guidance. A presumption means that a case should be decided in a certain way unless there are reasons to the contrary. A yardstick means exactly the same thing.

Why did Lord Nicholls feel the necessity to draw what is, in reality, a non-existent distinction? The answer, presumably, is that he himself was aware of the necessity for a fig-leaf to disguise the blatant fact that new law was being made.

It is paradoxical that in *White* itself the Law Lords themselves did not make equal awards. They upheld the Court of Appeal's decision that the wife should have assets worth £1.5 million with the husband retaining the remaining assets worth around £3 million. How was this inequality justified? By the fact that part of the assets had come from the husband's inheritance? As to this Lord Cooke commented that 'its significance was diminished because of the long marriage'. On the other hand Lord Nicholls mentioned the inheritance as a factor which the Court of Appeal had rightly taken into account. In the end the inequality was upheld on the simple ground that the Court of Appeal's award was 'well within the ambit of its discretion'.

Following the *White* decision I wrote articles about it in various legal journals and also for *The Times* law page. Mrs White herself saw *The Times* piece and wrote to me. She, it emerged, was by no means content with her award. It seemed to her (as it does to others) that having made the ringing declaration of principle, the Lords had lamentably failed to apply it in her case.

In *White* the Law Lords stated another principle which was not novel, save to the extent that it was offered as a justification for applying the equality 'yardstick'. Lord Nicholls put it thus:

> There is one principle of universal application which can be stated with confidence. In seeking to achieve a fair outcome there is no place for discrimination between husband and wife and their respective roles. Typically a husband and wife share the activities of earning money, running their home and caring for their children… If in their different spheres, each contributed equally to the family, then in principle it matters not which of them earned the money and built up the assets. There should be no bias in favour of the money-earner and against the home-maker and child-carer.

Section 25 itself requires the court to take into account the wife's contribution 'by looking after the home or caring for the family'. No-one has ever argued that this contribution should be minimised. But neither should it be maximised to the extent that *in itself* it would justify an equal division of assets. One problem lies in evaluating the homemaker's contribution as opposed to the breadwinner's. In the latter case, the contribution can be assessed objectively. If Mr Smith worked for 25 years and in the course of that time built up assets worth £1 million there can be no argument about the extent of his contribution. This is not true of a domestic contribution. There are bad as well as good wives. The husband might argue that his wife had been serially unfaithful, an absent housekeeper and an indifferent mother. Or he might say that he had provided helps and nannies which had enabled her to spend the years of the marriage doing little more than lunching and shopping. But arguments of this kind would be precluded by the Denning doctrine in *Wachtel*. Every family practitioner knows that the family courts hate issues of misconduct to be raised. District Judges are particularly unsympathetic to conduct allegations. Such allegations take time to investigate and the average District Judge's substantial daily caseload puts time at a premium. Since *White* the courts have held that the husband's special contribution to the creation of joint assets might be a factor justifying inequality of outcome. However, 'special contribution' has been so narrowly defined as to be a factor in only the most exceptional cases. To approach the matter otherwise would be (horror!) to 'fall into the trap of gender discrimination' (Lord Justice Thorpe in *Lambert-v-Lambert* ([2003] 1 FLR 142). In the *Lambert* case the Court of Appeal held that 'a good idea, initiative, entrepreneurial skill and extensive hard work' were insufficient to establish an 'exceptional contribution'. Lord Justice Thorpe went on to deprecate the practice of arguing for a special contribution, and referred with approval to the *Wachtel* precedent. In *Wachtel* Lord Denning had ruled that marital breakdown was in nearly all cases to be attributed to misfortune rather than misconduct. In the same way the acquisition of wealth should be assumed to have been the result of the joint endeavours of the parties and the court should not be interested in hearing arguments to the contrary.

It will be evident that the doctrine of equality so formulated is very attractive to a party whose actual contribution (as opposed to the notional and it might be entirely fictional contribution presumed by the court) has been routine or minimal.

Since the ruling in *White* London has acquired the reputation as a preferred forum for divorcing wives. It is easy to see why. If the rules themselves are biased, so is their application. The advice to be given to a husband thinking of litigating in the family courts, therefore, is simple enough: 'The law is against you. The culture is against you. Every presumption is in your wife's favour. Settle, therefore, on the best terms you can.'

No Escape! Contracting Out

In non-matrimonial contexts, it is a fundamental principle of English law that contracts entered into by sane and sober adults are binding. This rule is subject to exceptions where there has been, for example, deception or undue influence or a significant disparity in bargaining power.

Is there any reason why matrimonial contracts should not, in principle, be equally binding? In many jurisdictions, of course, prenuptial agreements are indeed enforceable and, among the very rich, commonplace. Ivana Trump cried off her intended second marriage because, so it was reported, her much less affluent husband refused to sign up—and very prudent of her too. In England, elaborate marriage contracts between wealthy parties were for centuries routine and a lucrative source of legal fees. To an eighteenth or nineteenth century court the notion that such an agreement should be any less binding than other contracts would have been strange.

The essence of a contract, of course, is that it contemplates the possibility that it might turn out badly for one of the parties who might then wish to resile from it. Freedom to contract, also, includes the freedom to make a disadvantageous or foolish bargain.

It is notorious, that under modern English matrimonial law, a matrimonial contract is not binding. It is merely one factor which the court will take into account when deciding how assets should be apportioned. This rule has two consequences. Firstly, there is little point in paying lawyers to draw up an elaborate agreement which in the end will probably not be enforceable. A legal agreement is designed to create certainty and this is the very thing a matrimonial contract does not achieve. Secondly, where there is (or is anticipated to be) a considerable disparity of wealth between the parties, the unenforceability of marriage contracts creates a strong disincentive for the richer party to get married at all.

A Footballer Saved From Drink

At this point we can consider the recently decided cases of McFarlane and Parlour ([2004] 2 FLR 895). Both cases went to the Court of Appeal and the judgements were handed down at the same time, the main judgement being given by our old friend Lord Justice Thorpe. It was the Parlour case which attracted media attention. The parties had met in February 1990 when the wife was a twenty-year-old employed by a local optician. Mr Parlour was only seventeen. He was a promising footballer and had signed a contract with Arsenal. He joined the Arsenal first team in January 1992 and in 1994 the wife gave up her employment. They began cohabiting in May 1995 and their first child was born in 1995, followed by a second in 1997 and a third in 1999. They did not, however, marry until June 1998. In November 2001 the marriage broke down and the husband left home.

Under an initial agreement made between the parties the wife took the matrimonial home described as 'a property of modest value in Norfolk' and a lump sum of £250,000. Her share represented about 37 per cent of the available capital assets. Shortly before the marriage breakdown however, the husband had signed a contract with Arsenal which produced average earnings of around £1.2 million net for the three years ending 2004/2005. In her evidence Mrs Parlour admitted that she herself had no earning capacity, that she had made no sacrifices in giving up her job at the opticians and that she had not been disadvantaged in staying at home. Finally she accepted that she had not given up any prospective career. This was not, therefore, a case where the Shakespeare/Mrs Shakespeare argument beloved of the family courts could be advanced. (If Shakespeare, rather than his wife, had been constrained to sit at home looking after the children and washing the socks it might well have been she who wrote King Lear.) The first instance Mr Justice Bennett nonetheless gave Mrs Parlour the kind of glowing reference to which we have become accustomed: 'There is no dispute, as I understand, that the wife was a marvellous mother and ran the household efficiently and looked after the children and husband to the very best of her considerable ability.'

But there was another significant contribution which the judge held Mrs Parlour had made: she had saved her husband from drink: 'I am satisfied that the husband was in an environment where before the advent of Arsene Wenger [a football coach m' lud] in 1996 there was very considerable drinking amongst certain players in the Arsenal football club. In the early days I am satisfied that the husband did participate in some of those drinking sessions. However, the wife realised that that was the way to ruin and unhappiness and I am satisfied that in or about the mid-1990s she took a grip on the situation and encouraged and persuaded her husband to move away from that style of living.' It is unclear from these words whether it was not in fact Mr Wenger who played the predominant part in Mr Parlour's salvation.

At all events the Court of Appeal seems to have accepted Mr Justice Bennett's findings of fact. It went on to make the further findings that the husband's income was likely to plummet within four or five years. That being the case the right result was to award Mrs Parlour net maintenance of £444,000 per annum which notionally would enable her to save £294,000 per annum as a reserve against the ultimate discharge of her Maintenance Order. The Appeal Court accordingly ordered the maintenance be paid for a four year *extendable* term. Thereafter, in the words of Lord Justice Thorpe 'Hopefully a clean break will be achievable then on an assessment of the husband's earning capacity at 35 years of age and the wife's independent fortune derived from the original capital settlement augmented by the substantial annual surplus built into her periodical payments order in the interim.'

It is worth analysing this result. Firstly, this was a short marriage and Mrs Parlour contribution amounted to no more than that of the routine input of the average wife (we may discount the guff about her role as temperance enforcer). If she had not had the pure good luck to marry a successful footballer she would presumably have set up with someone whose earning capacity was similar to her own as a shop assistant. The marriage to Mr Parlour, therefore, was very like purchasing a winning lottery ticket. The husband's contribution was, by any standards, wholly exceptional. Not many 30-year-olds earn £1 million a year.

Nonetheless, Mrs Parlour receives an award entirely based on the Family Courts' fiction that her contribution is to be assessed as equal to his (otherwise, God forbid, we might be witnessing discrimination).

And that is not the end of the matter. The £444,000 per annum Maintenance Order is extendable at the end of the four year term. At that time is it likely that Mrs Parlour will be content with her winnings to date? Or is it more probable that she will try to pluck another golden apple from this very fruitful tree? In that event Mr Parlour can contemplate further very expensive litigation before ... whom? Hayward Smith? Wilson? Singer? Thorpe? If not these, then people like them. Not exactly a level playing field. Poor old Parlour!

One can argue about the justice or otherwise of the result in *Parlour*. What is indisputable is that if any man in Mr Parlour's position had foreseen what was going to happen he would have wished to protect himself by

'You're SKINT and you know you are!'

means of a prenuptial agreement. And if he were told that such an agreement would not be enforceable he would, if in his right mind, not marry at all.

In relation to enforceability, matrimonial contracts are of two types, those made at the outset of the marriage (prenuptial agreements) and those intended to regulate the parties' position on its termination.

Prenuptial Agreements: Sorry, They Don't Work

There is a great wealth of authority that prenuptial agreements are not enforceable as such being (as we have seen) merely a factor to be taken into account in the post-breakdown litigation.

In the *F-v-F* case (where the wife claimed £4,000 per annum for the upkeep of her labrador) there was a prenuptial agreement. Of this Mr Justice Thorpe commented: 'It is not in dispute that contracts of this sort are commonplace in the society from which the parties come [Mr and Mrs F were of German origin] ... in this jurisdiction they must be of very limited significance. The rights and responsibilities of those whose financial affairs are regulated by statute cannot be much influenced by contractual terms which were devised for the control and limitation of standards that are ... of universal application throughout our society.' (He should more accurately have said 'standards laid down by over the years by right thinking chaps like me'.)

Nothing could be clearer than this. No matter what the circumstances, no matter how mature and well advised the parties, the courts treat them as children who cannot be trusted to make their own arrangements. Mr Justice Thorpe suggests that it is the 1973 Statute which prevents the Court from upholding prenuptial agreements, but he himself has emphasised the plenitude of the discretion given by the Act to the judges. The courts themselves have upheld prenuptial agreements when they wanted to (e.g. in the case of *K-v-K* ([2003] 1 FLR 120). It is only a single step from saying that sometimes a prenuptial agreement should be given weight to holding that they should always be binding in default of some overwhelming reason to the contrary. That would be on the assumption that the agreement was entered into under full legal advice to both parties and that there was no suggestion of undue influence or improper pressure.

Post Termination Agreements: They Don't Work Either

Following the breakdown of a marriage, the parties occasionally enter into a formal separation agreement. Far more frequently, however, they negotiate settlement terms intended to be embodied in a formal 'Consent Order' and presented to the court for approval. A Consent Order once made is binding and can only be set aside on proof of deception or non-disclosure of financial means. What, however, is the status of an agreement which has not been embodied in a formal Order? Here the attitude of the courts has been contradictory. On the one hand, they have declared that an agreement made after proper financial disclosure and with full legal advice ought to be upheld. There is, however, another (and more typical) strand of authorities which emphasise that draft Consent Orders ought not to be rubber stamped by the court. On the contrary, they should be properly scrutinised and rejected if thought inappropriate. In these authorities we see the courts' deep reluctance to accept that a grown-up person properly advised is entitled to make his/her own agreement, even an agreement which to others might look disadvantageous. This kind of thinking was well expressed by Sir Roger Ormrod in the case of *Camm-v-Camm* ([1983] 4 FLR 577):

> I bear fully in mind the natural feeling of the husband that if his former wife chooses to accept disadvantageous terms she cannot complain. That is not and never has been the way the law

approaches these matters, for the reason that agreements which are made in the throes of divorce are notoriously unreliable. It is not reasonable, generally speaking, to treat such agreements as if they were commercial bargains made by two people at arm's length with equal bargaining powers. The fact is that the emotional stresses, strains and urgencies of the situation may lead to grave misjudgements.

Yet again one must follow judicial reasoning to its logical conclusion. There can be very few divorces where both parties do not suffer from emotional stresses and strains. This being so, it must follow that very few agreements should be held final and binding. And why should the position be any different even if the agreement had been embodied in a formal Consent Order?

In *Camm* the parties separated and divorced in 1975 and entered into a financial settlement at about the same time. Five years later Mrs Camm applied, in effect, for the settlement to be set aside. She succeeded on the grounds that she had accepted 'in a position of great distress an arrangement which is manifestly unsatisfactory from her point of view'.

It is not surprising to discover that husbands cannot expect to be treated with the same indulgence as the wife in *Camm*. In *H-v-H* ([1993] 2 FLR 35) the wife had obtained an exceptionally generous Order by Consent. Under its terms she was to have a large lump sum, a car regularly replaced and periodical payments during joint lives. In the event that she remarried these payments would continue for a further ten years. This latter provision is virtually unprecedented. It is astonishing that the husband agreed it and that the original judge approved it.

In due course the husband fell on hard times and applied for a variation of the Order. In the course of the arguments (before Mr Justice Thorpe!) he submitted that the 1982 agreement could be re-opened on the ground that 'he had negotiated under intense emotional pressures'. Mr Justice Thorpe dismissed this argument with contempt—

notwithstanding that at the time of the original Order the husband was without legal representation, though in Thorpe's words he was 'manifestly in need of specialist solicitors and Counsel'.

It is not unfair to speculate that if Mrs H had entered into a manifestly unfair and oppressive agreement negotiated without legal assistance her plea for the court's indulgence would have been received rather more sympathetically.

Coming Back for More

In 1984, after a public outcry, a provision was inserted in the 1973 Matrimonial Causes Act requiring the court in making a financial Order to exercise its powers so that 'the financial obligations of each party towards the other will be terminated as soon after the grant of the Decree as the court considers just and reasonable'. The court was also given power to make a periodical payments Order 'for such a term ... as will in the opinion of the court be sufficient to enable the party in whose favour the Order is made to adjust without undue hardship to the termination of his or her financial dependence on the other party'. Following these amendments it became the general practice for District Judges to make clean-break Orders. These Orders were the easier to justify since in the average case the husband simply does not have sufficient income to provide worthwhile continuing maintenance for his ex-wife. The customary Order, therefore, might provide for the transfer of the bulk of the capital assets (usually only the former matrimonial home) to the wife leaving the husband with a continuing maintenance obligation only to the children. In the big money cases, too, periodical payments Orders fell out of fashion and it became the practice of the courts to capitalise the wife's maintenance entitlement over a period of years and to award a lump sum in lieu.

Following the decision in *Parlour-v-Parlour* it seems that we may be witnessing a revival of periodical payments Orders. In *Parlour* the term of the Order was four years but this was extendable. In *McFarlane* the total capital assets were £3 million of which the wife's agreed share was £1.5 million. In addition, she received maintenance of £250,000 per annum for an extendable term of five years. The justification for what to others might seem extravagantly large awards was the need and right of the wife to have enough income to save for her old age within the initial term of the maintenance Order. But the very fact that both Orders were made extendable admits the possibility that the wife would not, for whatever reason, put enough money aside. In that event, she would go back to the court for more, confident in the expectation that her explanations would receive a sympathetic hearing.

From time to time the Family judges themselves acknowledge that a powerful reason for imposing a clean break is to put an end to warfare between embittered ex-spouses. What could be more calculated to foment continuing discord than Orders of the type made in *Parlour* and *McFarlane*?

A periodical payments Order once made, upon what grounds should it be varied? District Judges generally work on the assumption that the original Order was correct and make an upward or downward variation to reflect any change in the parties' circumstances. This practice, however, is by no means an established rule and by no means to be relied on. As always, the courts have emphasised their unfettered discretion to do what they think is fair. In *Hall-v-Hall* we saw a grotesque example of the way in which this discretion can be exercised (that was the case where the wife stabbed her ex-husband in the stomach following which her continuing maintenance from him was merely *reduced*). In the equally grotesque decision in *Fisher*, the husband's maintenance obligation was sustained on the ground that the ex-wife needed the money for the support of the child she had conceived by another man following the breakdown of the marriage. Or take *Atkinson* where the wife admitted that she was not marrying her new cohabitee because she wished to continue receiving the handouts from her former husband. In the Court of Appeal Mr Justice Waterhouse reminded us that 'the tendency of the law has been to ensure that a woman does not have the right to maintenance from two men at the same time'. Moreover, she was entitled to spend her maintenance money on her boyfriend if she wished: 'How she spends her money was her affair ... it was just as irrelevant that she should be spending part of her money upon Mr Black [the boyfriend] as if she decides to have living with her an impecunious friend or an elderly relative'.

Finally, Mr Justice Waterhouse added: 'I am not impressed by the argument that the result of all this is to make the law appear to be an ass.' The idea!

Twenty Years On

In *Twiname-v-Twiname* ([1992] 1 FLR 29) the parties had married in 1940 and the marriage broke down in 1961. Mrs Twiname issued divorce proceedings in 1967 and maintenance was agreed in 1969. The Decree Nisi was finally pronounced in 1974. It was found that the husband had 'faithfully' paid the maintenance over a period of 20 years. In 1988 he sold his business whereupon the wife made a further application seeking a lump sum payment and an increase in maintenance. The husband argued that it would be wrong for a lump sum to be ordered after such a delay. In most other legal contexts a delay of this magnitude would indeed present a considerable obstacle. In *Twiname*, however, the Court of Appeal laid down the principle that 'however long the parties remain alive after the divorce, it is still open to one or other of them to make an application to the court'. So there was the unfortunate Mr Twiname, separated since 1961, with his ex-wife was still pursuing him for money over 30 years later. By virtue of what rational principle she should have been allowed to do so it is hard to discern.

Smashing Up the Happy Home

In *B-v-B* ([1995] 1 FLR 9)—a decision of Mr Justice Thorpe (again)—the parties had commenced cohabitation in 1975 and married in 1984. Almost from the beginning the marriage was unsuccessful and in 1986 each was consulting solicitors with a view to divorce proceedings. In 1987 there was what Mr Justice Thorpe described as a 'regrettable episode at the matrimonial home when the wife got drunk and smashed up the house'. (How would this incident have been described had it been Mr B who had behaved in this way?) In due course the solicitors for the parties negotiated a clean-break settlement under which the wife received 41 per cent of the joint assets and periodical payments diminishing over seven years. Before then Mrs B, in the words of the judge, 'drove to her husband's offices, smashed through gates, gained access to the office and smashed it up'. The husband, on the other hand, according to the judge, had 'throughout behaved extremely responsibly and with commendable restraint' and 'honourably throughout'.

The settlement negotiated between the parties was embodied in a Consent Order. The Order, as it emerged, was defective in that it contained no bar to applying for an extension. Mrs B accordingly made her application for upward review. It had admittedly been the intention of everyone involved that the Order should *not* be capable of extension. The husband, therefore, was asking no more than that an agreement freely negotiated by lawyers should be sustained. Some hope! In the words of Thorpe: 'The wife's needs are to me extremely clear. I think she needs financial support for her life.' So saying he increased the maintenance payments from £25,000 per annum to £33,000 to operate during joint lives or until the wife's remarriage. This case was decided less than ten years ago so it may be that Mr B is still paying.

In *Cornick-v-Cornick* ([1995] 2 FLR 490) the Court of Appeal approved this passage from an earlier Judgement:

> While I have regard to the fact that the parties have been divorced for 12 years and that much is undoubtedly due to the husband's unremitting hard work and effort, it is right that after 18 years of marriage the wife should also enjoy some part of the success and should have a standard of living commensurate with the situation as it now is.

Now there is some rationality in the argument that on the breakdown of a marriage the parties should share in each other's financial success. The notion (albeit often a fiction) is that each has contributed to that success. But what argument can there be for giving a divorced spouse a share of wealth acquired well after the breakdown?

In the *Richardson* case Mr Justice Thorpe found that 'the present disparity between the financial circumstances [of the husband and wife] is in part the product of the wife's mismanagement of her independent financial affairs'. In the event, however, that made no difference to the outcome and Mrs Richardson's application for extension of the duration of the maintenance Order was granted. Compare Thorpe's attitude in *Richardson* with the stern line he took in *Campbell-v-Campbell*([1988] 1 FLR 828). This was an appeal by a husband who had been ordered to pay maintenance to his wife for an indefinite period. The husband appealed on the ground that he simply could not afford to make the payments and presented a budget in support of his argument. He obtained short shrift from Lord Justice Thorpe in the Court of Appeal: 'It could be said that it would have been better if the judge had made a critical appraisal of the husband's presented budget and made specific findings as to which of the individual items asserted were reasonable and which were not.' However, he went on 'it has never been the custom in ancillary relief litigation to look with scrupulous care at the budget items of the prospective payer'. The husband had argued that his present expenditure included the provision of a home for his adopted children. Of this, Thorpe said 'his obligations in regard to those children, however excellent the motivation, were nonetheless voluntarily assumed'. As for the husband's debts, 'where there is pending litigation and one party incurs borrowing it is obvious that the running cost of servicing the borrowing cannot be prayed in aid against the other party who has managed his or her affairs without recourse to a loan'.

Legitimate Expectations

The law has been thrown into even greater confusion (if that were possible) by the recent Court of Appeal decision of *Miller-v-Miller* ([2005] EWCA CIV 984). Here the parties met in 1995 and became engaged in 1999, though they never co-habited. The marriage, which took place in 2001, was not a success, and in April 2003 the husband went off with another woman whom he subsequently married. There were no children.

At the time of the marriage Mrs Miller was a professional woman with an annual salary of £85,000, living in rented accommodation. The husband was in an altogether different league of affluence, earning £1million a year. At the time of the marital breakdown his assets amounted to approximately £17 million.

In due course Mrs Miller made her application for a lump sum. How much should she reasonably expect? Her husband's counsel based his argument on what was then thought to be the law, *viz* that, after a very short marriage to which the wife had made no significant financial contribution, she should in effect be awarded a sum of money sufficient to return her to her former position, to compensate her for any demonstrable loss she had suffered as a result of the marriage and also to 'put her back on her feet'.

Applying these criteria, Mr Miller at one point offered a settlement worth £1.3 million. In the event Mr Justice Singer awarded her £5 million. I will not attempt to plough through the morass of Singer's reasoning in arriving at this result. This task caused even the Court of Appeal some difficulty (Lord Justice Thorpe [inevitably!] complaining that he had had to search hard for the 'true ratio' of the first instance judge's decision.) In making his award Singer had laid stress on the wife's 'legitimate expectation' that in entering the marriage she would 'on a long term basis be living on a higher economic plain'. The Appeal Court agreed with this approach and upheld the award.

The concept of 'legitimate expectation' as a factor in adjudicating matrimonial financial disputes is entirely novel. Like 'discrimination' it is not a concept to be found either in the Matrimonial Causes Act 1973 nor in any of the cases decided in the 30 years or so following the Act.

In the Miller case it is interesting that the court should have allowed the wife to place reliance on her husband's alleged misconduct in support of her arguments for an enhanced award. We have seen that in the *Wachtel* case, Lord Denning had declared that, save in the most exceptional circumstances, the court should take no account of conduct, the notion being that marital breakdown was to be regarded as a misfortune rather than an event for which either party should be punished. The Denning approach has been followed more or less consistently ever since—or rather, I should say, consistently when applied against husbands, less so when invoked against wives. Here is the Denning doctrine as restated by Thorpe:

There must surely be room for the exercise of a judicial discretion between the pole of a wife who is driven to petition by the husband's unfeeling misconduct and that of a wife who exits from a marriage capriciously and for her own advantage.

But the Denning doctrine rests mainly on the presumption that it is hardly ever feasible to establish the rights and wrongs underlying a marriage breakdown. How many people are going to admit that they had driven out their spouse by 'unfeeling misconduct'? How many people are going to admit that they left a marriage 'capriciously'? And in default of an admission (or 'obvious and gross misconduct') how are the true facts to be established?

I am not concerned to argue about the justice or otherwise of the decision in *Miller*. As usual I let the facts speak for themselves. What, however, is undeniable is that the decision represents a huge deterrent to a marriage between parties where there is a considerable disparity of wealth. Would Mr Miller (or anyone else in his position) have married if he had been told: 'If, after three years, the marriage breaks down, your wife will walk off with a third of your assets. This is the contract you are making. Is that what you intend?'

Some family judges are aware that the marriage contract as interpreted by them is not wholly attractive to the party likely to be paying rather than receiving. This is why there is a movement to apply a quasi-matrimonial jurisdiction to cohabiting couples. From Lord Justice Thorpe and his strange justice there would then be no escape.

10

Summary

The state of the law in matrimonial financial disputes as illustrated by the cases I have discussed is as follows:

- There is a deep pro-wife bias with every single presumption in her favour—the most egregious being that every wife's contribution to the marriage is deemed to be equal to that of the husband even when plainly the contrary is true.

- The meal-ticket-for-life principle continues to flourish. A divorced wife has a continuing claim on her ex-husband until such time as he can find a sufficient capital sum to pay her off or alternatively some other man by way of marriage (cohabitation not being enough) assumes the obligation.

- Since *White-v-White* the courts (or rather, a tiny number of individual judges) have 'developed' the law to an extent amounting to virtual new legislation. The guiding principles now applied are the achievement of 'equality' and non-discrimination. These are concepts not to be found in the Matrimonial Causes Act and were hardly mentioned (if at all) before *White-v-White*.

- In particular cases (*Clark-v-Clark* being the best example) the justice applied by the courts would not be recognisable as such to anyone else. The injustice dispensed over the years is so routine and the mindset responsible for it so entrenched that it can fairly be described as institutional.

- The costs of matrimonial litigation are wholly disproportionate and occasionally, as even the courts admit, outrageous. These costs are largely the consequence of the uncertainty in the law, an uncertainty begotten by the almost unlimited discretion the judges claim for themselves in dealing with cases.

- In apportioning assets and making financial orders the courts have generally refused to take conduct into account, save in the most extreme circumstances. This means that a party who has repudiated all the obligations of the marriage can claim the financial benefits accruing from it to the same extent as if he/she had behaved impeccably. This rule is sometimes carried to extraordinary lengths—as in *Hall-v-Hall*—the stomach stabbing case. (It appears from the recent *Miller-v-Miller* decision that conduct might be making a comeback but only, we can be sure, if it is a question of the husband's misbehaviour rather than the wife's.)

11

Children

For some years campaigning fathers' groups have attracted media attention. Recently some of these groups have resorted to what they call direct action. Direct action has included dressing up as Batman, occupying court rooms and maintaining noisy vigils outside the houses of Family Division judges.

The fathers who have behaved in this way have attracted scant sympathy in the left-liberal press. On the contrary, they have been denounced as infantile exhibitionists whose alleged concern for their children was probably not genuine in any case. More probably, what we are seeing is desperate men behaving like desperate men. Groups like Fathers 4 Justice are a very recent phenomenon. Before them organisations like Families Need Fathers campaigned for years in the conventional manner. They circulated literature, lobbied judges and MPs and wrote to the newspapers. All their efforts, as we shall see, got them nowhere at all. The left-liberal press sneered at them too. The judges continued to insist that all was well and that the real problem was simply that the public was unaccountably failing to appreciate what an excellent job they were doing. Herself harried by Fathers 4 Justice, the Family Division President Dame Elizabeth Butler-Sloss assured a House of Commons select committee that the system operated no bias against fathers: 'There is nothing in the law that leans to choosing one parent or another.'

Bad Advice
Even the most complacent family judge, however, would have to acknowledge that there is a widespread perception

of bias and virtually all the anecdotal evidence points in that direction. One example: a year or two ago I acted for a divorcing father (Mr X) whose wife had gone to live with another man taking their three-year-old son with her. The other man happened to be a violent criminal with convictions for serious assaults. Mr X was worried about this and said he would like to apply for custody of his son (in legal parlance a residence order). His friends, however, had told him he would be wasting his time since fathers always lost custody disputes. No, no, I advised him. It was true that in general fathers did not do too well in the courts but this case was plainly in a different category. So Mr X issued his custody application with a supporting witness statement dealing in particular with the violent criminal's unsuitability as a step-father.

The application came before a part-time circuit judge whose function it was to set a date for a full hearing and make any consequential directions. I rose to make the application with Mr X behind me. The deputy circuit judge (whom I knew personally and with whom I was on friendly terms) frowned severely: 'Well Mr Mears, it's only fair to tell you that I am going to take some convincing before I take this little boy away from his mother.'

So the advice I had given the client was wrong and that he had received from his friends was right—or that, at least, was what Mr X concluded. He abandoned the case.

This is one of those anecdotes which, because of its inherent implausibility, people are reluctant to believe. Once again, then, let us turn to the law reports for confirmation of just how badly fathers fare.

Ending in Tears

The case of *Re D* ([2004] 1 FLR 1226) came before a well known family judge Mr Justice Munby in April 2004. This is what Munby said in delivering his judgement:

On 11 November 2003 a wholly deserving father left my court in tears having been driven to abandon his battle for contact with his seven-year-old daughter... Those who are critical of our family justice system may well see this case as exemplifying everything that is wrong with the system ... There is much wrong with our system and the time has come for us to recognise that fact and to face up to it honestly. If we do not we risk forfeiting public confidence. The newspapers—and I mean newspapers generally, for this is a theme taken up with increasing emphasis by all sectors of the press—make uncomfortable reading for us. They suggest that confidence is already ebbing away. We delude ourselves if we dismiss the views of journalists as unrepresentative of public opinion...

Here we have a very rare judicial admission of reality. The actual facts in *Re D* represented only an extreme example of injustices which for years have been commonplace. Mr D himself was described by one judge as 'a genuine and sincere father who loves his daughter and has her interest very much at heart'. A consultant clinical psychologist had described him as 'a balanced, fairly well integrated man' adding 'I found the father's interactions with his daughter to be indicative of a warm, caring relationship'. The mother, on the other hand, was described by the judge as 'obstructive, giving numerous unreasonable excuses why it was not appropriate to make the child available for contact... The mother constantly disobeyed contact orders from the court.'

Later on the judge referred to this obstructionism as amounting to 'sabotage'. The 'sabotage' continued over a period of five years despite court orders, penal notices, suspended prison sentences and eventually a period of 14 days imprisonment. During the litigation there were 43 hearings conducted by 16 judges. The parents' and experts' evidence totalled 950 pages.

What is astonishing is that Mr D continued the fight for so long. For most people the strain would have been unendurable: the knowledge that when you arrive for a pre-arranged contact visit you are likely to find the front door locked and the curtains drawn; or the child has suddenly been taken ill; or she can't see you because she has a piano lesson; or she is out playing with her friends and can't be interrupted. The variety of excuses used to frustrate a contact visit is infinite. And even if the visit happens to go ahead the father may wonder whether it is all worth the trouble. Under the first contact order, for instance, Mr D was allowed to see his daughter every Saturday between 10.00 a.m. and 5.45 p.m. Seven months later this was varied to allow weekly contact for two hours at a contact centre. The two-hour weekly contact was further varied to provide for supervision by a Court Welfare Officer. It is hard to see the value of 'contact' of this kind either to the parent or the child. It is more reminiscent of visiting time at the local hospital or prison.

In the continuing litigation which took place between June 1999 and February 2001 Mr D never succeeded in obtaining more than the two hours weekly contact at a contact centre. It was only in March 2001 that this contact was increased to seven. Since the father had initially been granted weekly unsupervised contact between 10.00a.m. and 5.45p.m., why was this so dramatically reduced? Mr Justice Munby gives the reason. It is, he said, 'the characteristic judicial response when difficulties with contact emerged: reduce the amount of contact and replace unsupervised with supervised contact'. In other words the mother is rewarded for her obstructionism. To quote Mr Justice Munby:

> Seen from a father's perspective, a case such as this exhibits three particularly concerning features:
>
> 1. The appalling delays of the court system, exacerbated by the absence of any meaningful judicial continuity, seemingly endless direction change, the lack of any overall timetable, and the failure of the court to adhere to such a timetable as has been set;
>
> 2. The court's failure to get to grips with the mother's groundless allegations; and
>
> 3. The court's failure to get to grips with the mother's defiance of its orders and the court's failure to enforce its own orders.

To read Munby's extensive judgement is to understand the context in which Fathers 4 Justice indulged in what their critics denounced as childish exhibitionism. No parent could have made greater efforts to obtain justice within the system than the father in *Re D*. In the event, as we have seen, five years and 43 hearings later he left the court in tears having obtained precisely nothing.

So why does the system work so badly? Part of the problem lies in what Munby himself called the 'flabby' attitude of the judges when faced with an obstructive parent: 'A flabby judicial response encourages the defaulting parent to believe that court orders can be ignored with impunity'.

But what explains the flabby response in the first place? In other contexts the courts are vigorous in asserting their authority and punishing overt disobedience. The answer again lies in the culture of the family judges. In this culture mothers are given the benefit of every doubt and there is a deep reluctance to acknowledge that contact difficulties may be down to simple ill will—perhaps there really was a misunderstanding over times; perhaps the child really did have a bad cold and had to go to bed; perhaps the piano lesson really did have to take priority because the teacher couldn't manage any other time...

To pursue his campaign at such length and in the face of so many obstacles and setbacks the father in *Re D* must have been something of an obsessive. He must also have been very rich or funded by legal aid. The cost of 43 hearings must have been staggering. Most fathers are neither very rich nor eligible for legal aid. Their ability to carry on the struggle, therefore, is severely handicapped by lack of money. Lacking the funds for legal representation, they have the alternative of giving up or of conducting the case in person via a system where they have every reason to believe the odds are stacked against them.

Mr Justice Munby indulged in an unwonted and extensive piece of breast beating over the deficiencies of the system but the remedies are in reality very simple. An obstructive parent should be given no more indulgence than any other disobedient litigant. Alternatively, she should be told in plain terms that if the obstructionism continues the court will accede to a custody (residence order) application from the other parent. If the courts adopted and were known to adopt this kind of robust position there is little doubt that the great majority of the so called 'intractable contact' disputes would be a thing of the past.

12

The Emigration Cases

Time and time again the courts have emphasised that their overriding concern is for the welfare of the child, the interests of the parents being a peripheral factor (if indeed to be considered at all). They have also declared repeatedly that parental contact is the child's right. If anyone doubted it, the emigration cases provide overwhelming evidence that what courts actually do is very different from what they say. Where there is a conflict between the interests of the child and those of the mother the reality is that it is those of the mother which nearly always prevail.

Following marital breakdown it is said that nearly 40 per cent of fathers lose contact with their children. One reason for this, as we have seen, is the mother's hostility to the father's continuing involvement. This is particularly so where she has found a new partner. It is an unfortunate fact also that many fathers lose interest in their children and make little attempt to keep in touch with them. Again, this is particularly common when the father enters into a new relationship. Finally, contact is likely to be lost when one of the parents moves away. I was involved in one case where a divorced father used every Saturday to drive from Norfolk to Devon to see his two small children between the hours of 10.30am and 5.30pm. He kept this up for some years. The mother had a new partner and would have been pleased had the contact visits stopped. Whenever the father was delayed *en route* and turned up late, even by ten minutes, he would find the visit had been cancelled altogether. Nonetheless he persevered. Many people in his position would eventually have given up.

If a distance of 200 miles represents a serious barrier to

continuing worthwhile contact the obstacle must be infinitely greater if one of the parents decides to emigrate. In practice there is every prospect that all contact with the other parent will be lost. In choosing to emigrate at all the custodial parent (nearly always the mother) makes it clear that she does not see continuing contact with the father as particularly valuable, still less a priority. If she decides to terminate contact altogether, or to make it as difficult as possible, the father has little practical remedy. The English court no longer has jurisdiction and his only legal recourse, therefore, is to litigate in a foreign country with all the enhanced uncertainty and expense that would involve.

Prima facie, therefore, and taking judicial talk about children's rights at face value, one would expect the courts' attitude to an emigration application from a custodial parent to be received unsympathetically. But the exact opposite is the case. There is a line of Court of Appeal decisions upholding a mother's right to emigrate with the children (or in legal terminology to remove them from the jurisdiction) in almost any circumstances.

Very Disappointed

In *Lonslow-v-Hennig (formerly Lonslow)* ([1986] 2 FLR 387) the two children involved were girls aged 12 and 10. Following their parents' divorce the mother remarried. In the Court of Appeal Lord Justice Dillon described the position as follows:

> The children had staying access every other weekend and during the holidays to their father and this has been very successful access. They kept clothes at the father's house ...so that in effect they had a second home there which they have enjoyed for many years. Furthermore, when they visit their father they see his parents, the parental grandparents of whom they are very fond. The judge [at first instance] said that it is a long, steady and profound relationship between the girls their father and their grandparents.

On these findings of fact, then, the position was just about as favourable to the non-custodial parent as it could be and it is hard to imagine what good reasons based on promoting the welfare of the children could exist for changing the situation.

At all events, the mother and her new husband decided to emigrate to New Zealand. She applied for leave to remove the children permanently and proposed that they should come to England every two years to visit their father for eight weeks or so during the school holidays. The father opposed the application contending that he would lose regular contact with the girls and that the maintenance of their close relationship with him was valuable to their welfare. The judge at first instance found that the mother's decision to emigrate was reasonable but concluded that the girls' important relationship with the father would be substantially disrupted and that, therefore, their interests were incompatible with the move to New Zealand. He consequently refused leave. The mother appealed to the Court of Appeal. She was successful. This was despite the fact that the appeal court has repeatedly said that it should not substitute its decision for that of the first instance judge who had the advantage of actually seeing the parties and 'feeling' the case (though, it need hardly be said, that this is a rule which the appeal court usually applies only when it happens to agree with the first instance decision).

What were the weighty reasons in *Lonslow* for depriving these children of their father? This is what Lord Justice Dillon said:

> The Hennigs [the mother had married Mr Hennig] decided that there were considerable advantages in emigrating to New Zealand. The Philips Group have a company in that country which was prepared to offer employment to Mr Hennig as a service engineer, in the first place at a salary similar to his present salary but in a country where money is thought to go further and where a good house can be obtained at a lower price than in this country ... the wish of Mr and Mrs Hennig to go with their family to New Zealand is a reasonable decision ... Mrs Hennig has, however, made it clear

'This court should not lightly interfere with such
reasonable way of life as is selected by that parent
to whom custody has rightly been given'

> that if she cannot take the children then she and Mr Hennig would
> stay behind in England ... She said that if that happened they would
> be very disappointed.

There is not much more to it than this. The children are to lose their father and Mr Lonslow his children because otherwise Mr and Mrs Hennig will not be able to take up a slightly better job in New Zealand causing them to be 'very disappointed'.

One must go on to discover why the court thought it so unreasonable to expect the custodial parent to cope with this disappointment. Lord Justice Dillon relied on passages from the earlier and similar case of *Poel-v-Poel* ([1970] 1 WLR 1469). The leading judgement there was given by Lord Justice Winn:

> When a marriage breaks up, the situation normally arises when the
> child of that marriage instead of being in the joint custody of both
> parents, must of necessity become one who is in the custody of a
> single parent. Once that position has arisen and the custody is
> working well, this court should not lightly interfere with such
> reasonable way of life as is selected by that parent to whom custody
> has been rightly given. Any such interference may ... produce
> considerable strains which would be unfair not only to the parent
> whose way of life is interfered with but also to any new marriage
> with that parent. In that way it might well in due course reflect on
> the welfare of the child. The way in which the parent who properly
> has custody of a child may choose in a reasonable manner to alter
> his or her way of life is one of those things which the parent who has
> not been given the custody may well have to bear, even though one
> has every sympathy with the latter on some of the results.

This reasoning is questionable in almost every respect. Firstly, there is the concentration on the rights of the custodial parent and her new partner, the interests of the children being introduced only as a kind of afterthought ('it might well in due course reflect on the welfare of the child'). Secondly, there is the assumption that whereas the children previously had two parents, they now somehow belonged to the custodial parent. Thirdly, there is scant interest in what the children themselves might think. The only reference to their possible view is Lord Justice Dillon's mention of the first instance judge's concern over their 'fear of the loss of their father'. This apparently would be offset by the higher salary the stepfather Mr Hennig would earn in New Zealand.

No consideration was given to the fact that, following an emigration of this kind, the children would not only lose the involvement of their father but also of their grandparents and other relations. They would be complete strangers in a new country. No one, of course, considered what the children's view of their new stepfather might be. Here another fiction of the family courts comes into operation *viz.* that children take readily to a new step-parent. The reality is that they are given no alternative.

Suppose Mrs Hennig and her new husband fell out while living in New Zealand? How would that affect the children?

The simple fact is that in *Lonslow* (as in the other emigration cases) children were being rooted up from a stable environment without the least regard to their own wishes. Deprived of their father and family, they are set down in a foreign land with a strange stepfather—and all this simply to indulge the mother's inalienable rights to live her life as she wishes.

Poel was decided in 1970 and *Lonslow* in 1986. At that time it was virtually the standard practice to make custody orders in favour of the mother, the father being 'granted' (revealing word) 'reasonable access'. In those days the courts did not think it necessary to pay even lip service to the rights of children. In recent years, however, residence/contact orders are only made in the minority of cases where the parties cannot come to their own agreement. At the same time the theory is promoted that residence/contact disputes should be decided purely in the interest of the children. One would have thought, therefore, that the modern Court of Appeal would view emigration applications in a different light. Not at all. Cultural bias is not so easily eradicated.

Off to Alabama

In *Re C* decided in 1998 ([1998] 1 FLR 848) the father appealed a decision by the County Court judge allowing the mother to take their six-year-old child to Alabama to live permanently with herself and her new American husband. It was found as a fact that the father had paid an unusually large role in caring for the child, having looked after her since the mother's return to full-time work when she was only six months old. After the separation the child lived with the mother but the father continued to play a large part in caring for her.

The father's appeal was dismissed on the ground that the judge had properly weighed the harm to the child of staying in England 'with the damage that would do to the mothers relationship' if permission to emigrate were refused. In this case the father's arguments made so little impression on the County Court judge that he did not bother to reserve his decision and refused leave to appeal. It appeared that the mother had made proposals for future contact with the father only to facilitate her emigration application. The new stepfather had 'adopted a regrettably combative approach' to the father. The reality, therefore, was that following the emigration this child would see very little if anything of her father. Did this matter? Apparently not. The court welfare officer's report spoke of the child's 'attachment to her father and her sadness at the prospect of leaving him'. Finally, the welfare officer had said that if the child went to live in the United States it was probable that she would suffer some measure of emotional damage. The mother, incidentally, had met the American gentleman only two years previously. So why was the application granted? Because 'the mother would have to rearrange her affairs to accommodate the situation. That would not be easy and it would be stressful for her.' And that was it.

... and off to Nigeria

The fiction that the courts' real concern is for the welfare of the children rather than the aspirations of the mother is conspicuously illustrated in *Re K* ([1998] 2 FLR 1006). Here, the parents were Nigerians but the children (aged nine and seven) had been brought up and educated in England. The children had a good relationship with both their parents and saw their father regularly.

The mother applied to take them to Nigeria on the grounds that she would be able to further her career as a teacher there and be in contact with her family and her new boyfriend. The boyfriend? Yes indeed. As to him, the judge said: 'I accept that a significant part of the mother's motivation is her wish to try and develop her relationship with her boyfriend.' Finally, the mother said that if she were not given permission to emigrate she would probably go to Nigeria in any event, leaving the children behind. Despite this she was given permission to emigrate on the usual ground. This was a mother who almost in explicit terms had told the court that if in the last resort she had to choose between her children and the boyfriend it would be the boyfriend who would come first.

Nigeria, of course, is an impoverished third-world country with a history of instability, corruption and lawlessness. How could it possibly be in the children's interest to send them there deprived of their father and in the hands of a mother who preferred their putative stepfather to them?

Shift in Perceptions?

In *Payne-v-Payne* ([2001] FLR 1052) the unfortunate father tried a new tack. Here the child at the date of the appeal was aged four and the mother (a citizen of New Zealand) was applying for permission to take her to reside in that country. The first instance judge described the child as 'healthy, intelligent, lively and happy', adding: 'She is devoted to both her parents and they love her. She has a strong attachment to the paternal grandmother and whilst she has seen comparatively little of the maternal grandmother over the past months I am sure that she has been no less attached to that lady.'

The father's counsel presented two main arguments. Firstly, he submitted that since *Poel-v-Poel* there had been a shift in perceptions. Some hope! In the words of the judge (Lord Justice Thorpe!): 'The shift upon which he relies is in the sphere of contact. He asserts that over the last 30 years the comparative importance of contact between the child and the absent parent has greatly increased.' This, one would have thought, would be the assertion of a commonplace. The desirability of maximum contact with both parents is the maxim frequently reiterated by the family judges themselves. But what did Thorpe say of it? 'No authority for the proposition is demonstrated. Without some proof of the proposition I would be doubtful of accepting it.' So here is the most senior family judge demanding specific authority to establish the proposition that a child should have maximum contact with both parents!

The father's second submission was that the *Poel* approach is incompatible with the Human Rights Act 1998 which incorporates the European Convention for the Protection of Human Rights and Fundamental Freedoms. Article 8 of the Convention reads: 'everyone has the right to respect for his private and family life ...' This provision is so vaguely worded that an argument based on it would be unlikely to succeed unless the tribunal was already predisposed to accept it. This, of course, was far from the case and the husband's appeal was dismissed on the usual *Poel* grounds.

Making the Mother Happy

In *Payne* the summary headnote in the Family Law Report described the true state of the law as expressed in the original decision (and upheld by the Court of Appeal): 'The judge gave the mother leave to remove the child permanently to New Zealand, applying the relevant case law and finding that the move would be in the child's best interests *because it would make her mother happy.*' (my italics)

In *Payne* Dame Elizabeth Butler-Sloss listed the theoretical factors governing the courts' attitude to an emigration application:

(a) The welfare of the child is always paramount
(b) There is no presumption in favour of the applicant parent
(c) The reasonable proposals of the parent with a residence order wishing to live abroad carry great weight
(d) Consequently, the proposals have to be scrutinised with care and the court needs to be satisfied that there is a genuine motivation for the move and not the intention to bring contact between the child and the other parent to an end
(e) The effect upon the applicant parent and the new family of the child of a refusal of leave is very important
(f) The effect upon the child of the denial of contact with the other parent and in some cases his family is very important
(g) The opportunity for continuing contact between the child and the parent left behind may be very significant

How are these factors applied in practice?

Factor (a)
It is said that the welfare of the child is the paramount

consideration. **Comment:** In practice, as we have seen, this welfare is equated with the mother's wishes.

Factor (b)

It is said that there is no presumption in favour of the applicant parent. **Comment:** This is manifestly untrue. In *Moodey-v-Field* (which we have already considered) Lord Justice Dillon said:

> It is, I must say, a proposition which strikes me with some surprise that a father should seek to hold his former wife in this country in order that she should continue to look after these children here, unless it is plainly very important indeed to those children that they should remain here. It seems to me, looking at this situation not only as a judge but as a human being, that he who puts forward such a proposal has a heavy burden to discharge.

What is a 'heavy burden to discharge' if not a presumption? It is interesting that Dame Elizabeth herself delivered the first instance judgement in *Moodey-v-Field*.

Factor (c)

It is said that the custodial parent's 'reasonable proposals' to emigrate 'carry great weight'. **Comment:** This is a gross understatement. The decided cases show that these proposals (reasonable or otherwise) are almost invariably the overriding factor. In nearly all the emigration cases the children are removed from a familiar, happy and secure environment to an alien scene where their future happiness must necessarily be speculative. In *Re K* the children were being taken from a rich, stable country to a poor unstable one (Nigeria). In that case it was easy to see why the mother wanted to depart but not why this could possibly benefit the children—save again on the supposition that the custodial parent's aspirations are coterminous with the children's interests. Here we can look at some of the most recent decisions:

A High-Risk Strategy

In *L-v-L* ([2003] 1 FLR 900) the mother applied for permission to take two children then aged four and three to the United States with her new husband. Mr Justice Johnson found as a fact that the children had a good relationship with the father and that he had played an active part in their lives.

The elder child had a learning disability and attended a specialist school. No less than three independent professional witnesses advised against permitting the removal of this child. One of the experts thought that 'going to America would be a high-risk strategy' and emphasised the significance of 'the close frequent support from her father that she is used to'. In the event the judge brushed aside the opinion of the expert witnesses as having 'overstated the risk'. He went on to say: 'Each of these three professionals focused on what they regarded as best for the [elder child] whereas I have to balance any perceived disadvantage or risk to [the elder child] against the disadvantage to the family and hence to the children if the mother's application is refused.'

'Large Adjustments'

In *Re C* ([2003] 1 FLR 1066) the familiar gross bias appears again. Here the applicant mother was a native of Singapore living in England and the two children were aged 11 and 8. The father was English and the children had been brought up entirely in England. English was their only language. The judge found as a fact that the children were attached to both parents and that the father was deeply concerned about their welfare. He added: 'The boys have interests and talents in, amongst other things, sport and music. They have a number of friends in this country. Notwithstanding the fact that their mother is Singaporean and they have visited Singapore regularly, this country is their home. It is clear that they will have to make large adjustments if they move to live in Singapore and their reaction to the changes they will have to face if they do so are uncertain.'

The judge went on to add that he agreed with the independent professional witness that 'the best solution would be for the boys to remain in this country living with the mother on the basis that changes are made that made the mother and the boys happier'. He listed the disadvantages of the removal to Singapore, *viz*:

(1) It would reduce the contact the boys enjoy with their father.
(2) It would introduce significant changes in their day-to-day lives which may cause them difficulties. These include changes in respect of schooling, activities, friends, weather and language.
(3) In Singapore the mother will face a number of the difficulties both practical and emotional that she faces here in rebuilding her life.
(4) The mother has now been away from Singapore for a long time and her old friends and acquaintances will be busy with their own lives. Also her parents do not speak English which will naturally make it difficult for them to build a relationship with the boys quickly.

So, having himself set out an abundance of excellent reasons for concluding that emigration would certainly *not* be in the children's interests, what did the judge do? He granted the mother's application but invited her to reconsider her position. For this bizarre decision the usual reason was advanced—if the mother's wishes were frustrated she would become unhappy and it was not in the children's interests that she should be so.

A Question of Infatuation
We have seen how in the emigration cases the courts make

decisions at variance with their own findings of fact and how the evidence of independent professionals is brushed aside. In *Re B* ([2003] 2 FLR 1043) the Court of Appeal disregarded its own familiar rule that (issues of law and manifest error aside) the first instance judge's exercise of his discretion should be upheld. It is he who has heard the parties and been able to assess face-to-face the quality of the evidence given by them and any other witnesses (including independent professionals).

In *Re B* and *Re S* two separate trial judges had refused the mother's applications to relocate.

In *Re B* the mother had formed an association with a South African and wished to take the two children (then aged 10 and 7) to South Africa. The trial judge O'Brien made the following comments on the application:

> There remains a serious query, to my way of thinking. It is undoubtedly the case that the mother's character is mercurial. The way she has described her relationship with Mr K has struck me as being that of the first fine careless rapture of a teenager... It is largely an untried, untested relationship. The pattern is that the parties have been together for short periods and then apart ... I ask myself from the point of view of the children, what would happen if it breaks down? Both parties spoke of having a child but neither of them has said anything about marriage. What is the security of mother and the children if they go to South Africa and things do not work out?... Mother has no friends and family of her own in South Africa... With neither party divorced, no proposal to remarry, very unclear as to what might happen, and an untried and untested relationship. I am concerned that from the point of view of the children these proposals are not realistic at present.

These comments amount, one might think, to simple common sense. The judge's reservations would apply in only too many of the emigration cases.

We need not, however, be surprised that in the Court of Appeal Lord Justice Thorpe adopted a different position. The trial judge's approach, he said, was 'plainly erroneous'. He added: 'Once the judge had recognised the mother as plainly the primary carer he had no option but to recognise the reality that her future lay with Mr K and that necessarily meant a South African future.' But the basis of Judge O'Brien's reservations was that it was by no means certain that the mother's future lay with Mr K. Having heard her evidence, he formed the view that she was, in effect, infatuated. He asked himself what would be the position of both mother and children if her infatuation (or that of Mr K, for that matter) should evaporate? These were the trifling concerns which Thorpe thought reflected an approach which was 'plainly erroneous'.

Factor (d)

It is said that the court needs to be satisfied that 'there is a genuine motivation for the move and not the intention to bring contact between the child and the other parent to an end'. **Comment:** As a determining factor this must in practical terms be illusory. No applicant is going to say, 'I have no good reason for emigrating. It's just that I can't stand my ex and want to get the children away from him.'

In the absence of such a confession, how is the court to determine true motivation? Moreover, the institutional bias of the family courts ensures that where there is a doubt about good faith the applicant will be given the benefit of it.

Factor (e)

It is said that 'the effect upon the applicant parent and the new family of the child of a refusal is very important'. **Comment:** Here again, no applicant is going to say in explicit terms: 'I would like to take the children abroad but if I am refused permission I won't too much mind and will make the best of things.' It is remarkable that judges who, after all, have spent most of their adult life as practising barristers should talk as though they were unaware that witnesses are coached. The evidence they give in court has previously been filtered by their legal advisors. Unless they are very stupid they are not going to say anything obviously likely to make a bad impression. Thus to the question: 'If you emigrate will you do your best to ensure that the children have maximum contact with their other parent during the holidays', the correct answer is 'Yes, there is nothing I am more anxious to ensure'. Such evidence will be believed even though it is transparently improbable—in *Re C*, as we have seen, the mother had made proposals for future contact with the father only to facilitate her emigration application and the new stepfather was on bad terms with the father. The plain reality, therefore, was that contact in that case was not going to be enthusiastically promoted by the custodial parent. Nevertheless, she was given permission to emigrate. We are in the presence of the presumption that the custodial parent is entitled to lead her life as she wishes and that if she is thwarted the welfare of the child is going to be affected. This presumption applies even when there is independent evidence that if emigration is permitted the risk of adverse consequences outweighs that of refusing it.

Factor (f)
It is said that the 'effect upon the child of the denial of contact with the other parent, and in some cases his family, is very important'. **Comment:** So it is. But in practical terms it is a factor to which the courts attach minimal weight. If it were otherwise there would be a series of cases where permission to emigrate had been refused. As it is, the decision in *Payne* demonstrates that any trial judge refusing permission, save in the most extreme circumstances, is going to be overruled by the Court of Appeal.

Factor (g)
It is said that 'the opportunity of a continuing contact between the child and the parent left behind may be very significant'. **Comment:** The opportunity for continuing

contact is affected by a number of factors. Firstly, there is the sheer inconvenience and cost involved. How frequently is it feasible for young children to travel from New Zealand and back again? How many parents can afford the airfares? Secondly, the absence of regular contact itself tends to break down old ties. And as these ties diminish so will the wish for contact, particularly on the part of young children. Thirdly, the contact will depend almost entirely on the goodwill of the custodial parent and her new partner. If this goodwill is absent the father's only option is to take legal action in the foreign jurisdiction. For the great majority of non-custodial parents this is not a practical option.

The Emigration Cases: Summary

The emigration cases establish overwhelmingly the existence of the deep-rooted bias of the courts in favour of the custodial parent (nearly always the mother). When the welfare of the child conflicts with the aspirations of the mother it is the latter which nearly always take precedence.

About the deep injustice inflicted on the non-custodial parent I have said nothing. That the injustice exists is never, of course, acknowledged by the courts themselves. This wrong affects equally the children rooted up without their consent. They lose their father, their family and their friends. They are transported to a foreign country to take their chances with a new step-parent—a country where (as in *Re C*) they may not even speak the language. And all this, we are told, is done for their benefit.

13

General Conclusions

I have examined the way in which the family courts have dealt and continue to deal with financial and children disputes. The decided cases, I hope, speak for themselves (*res ipsa loquitur*, as the lawyers put it). They represent, I have argued, an institutional injustice. In the case of financial disputes the injustice is exacerbated by uncertainty. Here the law as applied by the courts has undergone (and continues to undergo) a continuing process of 'development'. The 'development', as we have seen, is all in one direction, culminating in the House of Lords decision in *White-v-White*. Even so, 'development' of this kind necessarily produces uncertainty. And uncertainty begets litigation and legal costs. It is no accident that the costs in *White* itself were so outrageous. Litigation is also the inevitable consequence of the extremely wide discretion which the courts claim for themselves. At District Judge level, it is particularly difficult to predict how the court will (to quote Lord Denning's notorious image) decide to take the pieces out of the bag and redistribute them between the parties.

Lord Denning thought the judges (and himself in particular) at least as well qualified as Parliament to make law. This is still the attitude of the family judges, albeit not so openly avowed. It might occasionally be acknowledged that a decision like that of Haywood Smith in *Clark-v-Clark* is less than perfect. Otherwise there is no sign that the courts have anything less than complete confidence in the woeful justice they dispense or in their own wisdom. Here there is a parallel with the succession of wrongful conviction cases (Birmingham Six, Guildford Four, Luton post office murder, etc.) which finally resulted in the establishment of the Criminal Cases Review Commission. Time and again the Court of Appeal was resolute in denying what was plain to almost everyone else—that a serious miscarriage of justice had occurred and needed urgent redress.

With children disputes, at least, there is some belated consciousness on the part of a few judges that all is not well. The stream of anecdotal evidence about the injustices routinely inflicted on fathers and children has been flowing too strongly to be disregarded in the old complacent manner. Mr Justice Munby's judgement in *Re D* was a milestone. It represented the first public acknowledgement by a senior family judge of what many litigants and their lawyers already knew, *viz*: the machine simply doesn't work. This was Munby's message, though it is very doubtful that it has yet filtered through to the Court of Appeal.

What can be done about reforming the system? The dispiriting answer is that very little change can be expected while the same few judges apply the same old rules according to the same old prejudices. It is the culture which needs changing. That takes time, although eventually the wheel will turn—particularly under the impact of sustained and vigorous criticism. Even very senior judges, for instance, now pay lip-service to the right of a child to maintain close contact with its father (although, as the emigration cases, show it *is* only lip-service).

This unfortunately is an area of law where legislative intervention by Parliament can have only a limited role. On marital breakdown no two financial situations are identical and it is inevitable, therefore, that the courts should be vested with a considerable degree of discretion in apportioning the assets. There is, however, no reason why strenuous efforts should not be made to curtail the scope of this discretion. Here it is a paradox that non-married cohabitees have complete freedom in making whatever financial agreement they think appropriate, whereas this is a liberty the courts insist on denying to spouses—Denning and his successors always know best.

Looking at the decisions of the English courts over the past ten years, it is not surprising that for wives married to rich husbands London now rivals California as the divorce forum of choice. Indeed, the pro-wife bias of English courts is now such that it is surprising that any rich man marries at all. In doing so he binds himself to a contract which, as interpreted by the courts, is in every respect one-sided. What other legal contract entitles one party to repudiate all its obligations while retaining all the rights? It is, as we have seen, difficult to construct legislation which is judge-proof. However, a reformed system would incorporate at least the following elements:

- Pre- and post-nuptial agreements entered into with proper legal advice should be fully binding. Such agreements would not affect the courts' power to make awards for the benefit (but solely for the benefit) of any children.
- In making a financial award any assets owned by one of the parties before the marriage should, save in exceptional circumstances, be disregarded on breakdown. The same would be true of an inheritance. Why should anyone profit from assets which he/she has done nothing to create?
- Spousal maintenance should not be awarded to a party who by his/her conduct has repudiated the marriage. This, in theory, is already the law (as set out in the 1984 amendment to the Matrimonial Causes Act 1973). It is, however, not the law as 'developed' by Denning & Co.
- The right of a child to maintain maximum contact with both parents should be recognised in fact as well as in principle. This means that a custodial parent would not, save in exceptional circumstances, have the right to move abroad.

Reforms along these lines would, of course, provide no complete panacea. Judges would retain a very wide measure of discretion. But some kind of start has to be made in reducing their ability to do harm and inflict injustice, and the sooner the better.